Managing Planet Earth

Managing Planet Earth

. . .

READINGS FROM
SCIENTIFIC AMERICAN MAGAZINE

W. H. FREEMAN AND COMPANY
New York

Cover image by George V. Kelvin

Library of Congress Cataloging-in-Publication Data

Managing planet earth : readings from Scientific American magazine.
     p.   cm.
   Includes bibliographical references.
   ISBN 0-7167-2108-2
   1. Nonrenewable natural resources — Management. 2. Economic
development — Environmental aspects. I. Scientific American.
HC59.M244   1990
333.7 — dc20   89-48324
                                                          CIP

The eleven chapters and the epilogue in this book originally
appeared as articles and the closing essay in the September
1989 issue of Scientific American.

Printed in the United States of America

2 3 4 5 6 7 8 9 0   RRD   9 9 8 7 6 5 4 3 2 1

CONTENTS

Foreword

Like bacteria exuberantly replicating in a petri dish, William Clark says, our species has exploited the substrate that is our planet with prodigious success. Only 10,000 years ago we comprised 5 to 10 million individuals scattered in neolithic settlements. By the middle of the 20th century we numbered 2.5 billion; sometime in 1987 we passed the 5 billion mark. That rate of growth, according to the laws of biology, may verge on being a capital offense. Populations of bacteria that outstrip resources stagnate and collapse as they submerge in their own wastes, Clark notes. We must conjure with the fact that our own biological success may have begun to produce a comparable situation. Air, water, climate and other forms of life have begun to suffer, perhaps irreversibly, from the effects of our economic activity. If such processes run unchecked, it seems highly probable that we will render our planet uninhabitable. Yet we cannot reasonably throw our economic engines into reverse. The population of the southern hemisphere demands the prosperity that the north enjoys; the north has committed itself to continued growth as the strategy for maintaining its standard of living. We must find ways then to reconcile our economy and the technologies that drive it with the great cycles of nature that sustain us. In the pages of *Managing Planet Earth* the creative and responsible scientists, administrators and managers explore strategies for achieving this vital balance. How well we succeed in implementing such policies will decide the fate of our species.

Jonathan Piel
For the Board of Editors

Managing Planet Earth

Managing Planet Earth

Introducing a book that explores the prospects for sustainable human development on a planet with finite resources and a fragile environment.

. . .

William C. Clark

Every form of life continually faces the challenge of reconciling its innate capacity for growth with the opportunities and constraints that arise through its interactions with the natural environment. The remarkable success of our own species in meeting that challenge is reflected in the striking image that graces the cover of this book. That initial success, however, is only the beginning of the story.

As we seek to imagine different ways in which that story might unfold, analogies can be helpful. The global pattern of light created by today's civilizations is not unlike the pattern of exuberant growth that develops soon after bacteria are introduced to a nutrient-rich petri dish. In the limited world of the petri dish, such growth is not sustainable. Sooner or later, as the bacterial populations deplete available resources and submerge in their own wastes, their initial blossoming is replaced by stagnation or collapse.

The analogy breaks down in the fact that bacterial populations have no control over, and therefore no responsibility for, their ultimate collision with a finite environment. In contrast, the same wellsprings of human inventiveness and energy that are so transforming the earth have also given us an unprecedented understanding of how the planet works, how our present activities threaten its workings and how we can intervene to improve the prospects for its sustainable development. Our ability to look back on ourselves from outer space symbolizes the unique perspective we have on our environment and on where we are headed as a species. With this knowledge comes a responsibility not borne by the bacteria: the responsibility to manage the human use of planet earth.

At the individual level, people have begun to respond to increased awareness of global environmental change by altering their values, beliefs and actions. Changes in individual behavior are surely necessary but are not enough. It is as a global species that we are transforming the planet. It is only as a global species—pooling our knowledge, coordinating our actions and sharing what the planet has to offer—that we have any prospect for managing the planet's transformation along pathways of sus-

Figure 1.1 MANAGING PLANET EARTH will require answers to two questions: What kind of planet do we want? What kind of planet can we get? To resolve these questions human beings must understand how their activities affect the global environment and must choose strategies for developing the planet. One local aspect of a possible global strategy is symbolized here by a Nepalese woman planting a tree as part of a reforestation project.

tainable development. Self-conscious, intelligent management of the earth is one of the great challenges facing humanity as it approaches the 21st century.

Although efforts to manage the interactions between people and their environments are as old as human civilization, the management problem has been transformed today by unprecedented increases in the rate, scale and complexity of those interactions. What were once local incidents of pollution now involve several nations—witness the concern for acid deposition in Europe and in North America. What were once acute episodes of relatively reversible damage now affect multiple generations—witness the debates over chemical- and radioactive-waste disposal. What were once straightforward confrontations between ecological preservation and economic growth now involve multiple linkages—witness the feedbacks among energy consumption, agriculture and climatic change that are thought to enter into the greenhouse effect.

We have entered an era characterized by syndromes of global change that stem from the interdependence between human development and the environment. As we attempt to move from merely causing these syndromes to managing them consciously, two central questions must be addressed: What kind of planet do we want? What kind of planet can we get?

What kind of planet we want is ultimately a question of values. How much species diversity should be maintained in the world? Should the size or the growth rate of the human population be curtailed to protect the global environment? How much climatic change is acceptable? How much poverty? Should the deep ocean be considered an option for hazardous-waste disposal?

Science can illuminate these issues but cannot resolve them. The choice of answers is ours to make and our grandchildren's to live with. Because different people live in different circumstances and have different values, individual choices can be expected to vary enormously. As pointed out by Gro Harlem Brundtland in the Epilogue, poor people and rich people are especially likely to place different values on economic growth and environmental conservation. Recently, however, the long-standing debate over growth versus environment has matured considerably. A broad consensus has begun to emerge

that interactions between people and their environments should be managed with the goal of sustainable development (see Figure 1.1).

The World Commission on Environment and Development (WCED), chaired by Prime Minister Brundtland, characterizes sustainable development as paths of social, economic and political progress that meet "the needs of the present without compromising the ability of future generations to meet their own needs." Sustainable development thus reflects a choice of values for managing planet earth in which equity matters—equity among peoples around the world today, equity between parents and their grandchildren.

Managing the planet toward sustainable development is an undertaking made no less daunting by its urgency. The basic human dimensions of the task are explored in Chapter 6, "The Growing Human Population," by Nathan Keyfitz, and in Chapter 10, "Strategies for Sustainable Economic Development," by Jim MacNeill. The broad picture, although familiar, bears recounting. The planet today is inhabited by somewhat more than five billion people who each year appropriate 40 percent of the organic material fixed by photosynthesis on land, consume the equivalent of two tons of coal per person and produce an average of 150 kilograms of steel for each man, woman and child on the earth. The distribution of these people, their well-being and their impact on the environment vary significantly among countries.

At one extreme, the richest 15 percent of the world's population consumes more than one third of the planet's fertilizer and more than half of its energy. At the other extreme, perhaps one quarter of the world's population goes hungry during at least some seasons of the year. More than a third live in countries where the mortality for young children is greater than one in 10 (see Figure 1.2). The vast majority exist on per capita incomes below the official poverty level in the U.S.

As we look to the future, it is encouraging that the growth rate of the human population is declining virtually everywhere. Even if the trends responsible for the decline continue, however, the next century will probably see a doubling of the number of people trying to extract a living from planet earth. Nearly all of the increase will take place in today's poorer countries. According to the WCED, a fivefold to tenfold increase in world economic activity dur-

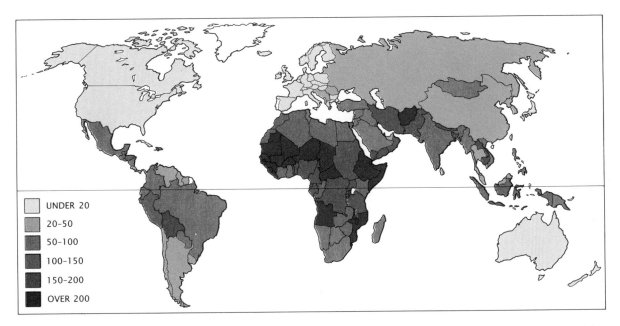

Figure 1.2 CHILD MORTALITY is one measure of a population's well-being. The map shows deaths per 1,000 live births for children younger than five years. More than one third of the world's people live in countries where the mortality is greater than one in 10. The data, estimated for 1985 to 1990, are from the U.N.'s Department of International Economic and Social Affairs.

ing the next 50 years will be required to meet the basic needs and aspirations of the future population. The implications of this desperately needed economic growth for the already stressed planetary environment are at least problematic and are potentially catastrophic.

Efforts to manage the sustainable development of the earth must therefore have three specific objectives. One is to disseminate the knowledge and the means necessary to control human population growth. The second is to facilitate sufficiently vigorous economic growth and equitable distribution of its benefits to meet the basic needs of the human population in this and subsequent generations. The third is to structure the growth in ways that keep its enormous potential for environmental transformation within safe limits—limits that are yet to be determined.

If the goals of sustainable development describe the type of planet people want, the second question still remains: What kind of planet can we actually get? When we address this question, the focus shifts from what we value to what we know.

In the end the strategies for sustainable development must translate into local action if they are to have any impact at all. As I have noted, however, many of today's most intractable challenges to sustainability involve time scales of decades or centuries and global spatial scales. Any significant improvements in our ability to manage planet earth will require that we learn how to relate local development action to a global environmental perspective.

Fortunately, understanding of global environmental change has been revolutionized in recent years. The revolution has its roots in the 1920's, with the Russian mineralogist Vladimir I. Vernadsky's seminal writings on the biosphere. It received important impetus from the International Geophysical Year of 1957 and is now being carried forward through a lively array of research and monitoring efforts around the world, capped by an ambitious new International Geosphere Biosphere Program. Although the "global change" revolution is far from complete, its broad outlines can be summarized in Figure 1.3.

The view of environmental change outlined in

Figure 1.3 shows a planet dominated through decades and centuries by the interactions of climate and chemical flows of major elements, interactions that are woven together by the global hydrological cycle and are significantly influenced by the presence of life.

The climate system incorporates atmospheric and oceanic processes that govern the global distribution of wind, rainfall and temperature. Processes central to human transformation and management of planet earth include changes in concentrations of greenhouse gases and their impact on temperature; the effect of ocean circulation on the timing and distribution of climatic changes; and the role of vegetation in regulating the flux of water between land and atmosphere (see Chapter 3, "The Changing Climate," by Stephen H. Schneider).

A second important component of the planet's environment is the global circulation and processing of major chemical elements such as carbon, oxygen, nitrogen, phosphorus and sulfur. These elements are the principal components of life. In chemical forms such as carbon dioxide, methane and nitrous oxide, they also exert a major influence on climate. Even in the absence of human influences, the earth's climate and chemistry have undergone abrupt and tightly linked changes such as those reflected in the ice-core records shown in Figure 3.3. When added to these natural fluctuations, human activities have created disturbances in global chemi-

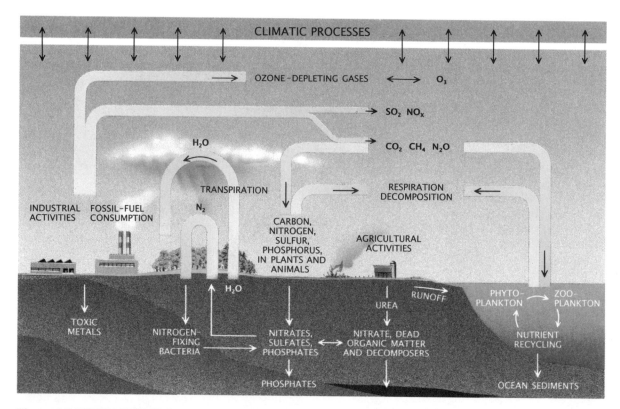

Figure 1.3 INTERACTIONS between the climate and major chemical flows dominate global environmental change over tens to hundreds of years. Water is taken out of the atmosphere by precipitation and returned by evaporation and transpiration. Human agriculture affects the planetary system by altering the flows of nitrates, phosphates and carbon compounds. Respiration and decompo-sition liberate methane (CH_4). The combustion of fossil fuels releases large quantities of stored carbon to the atmosphere as CO_2 which like CH_4 tends to warm the planet. Emissions such as sulfur dioxide (SO_2) and nitrogen oxides (NO_x) are important causes of acid rain. Industrial emissions of gases like the chlorofluorocarbons (CFC's) deplete ozone (O_3) and also contribute to climatic change.

cal flows that manifest themselves as smog, acid precipitation, stratospheric ozone depletion and other problems (see Chapter 2, "The Changing Atmosphere," by Thomas E. Graedel and Paul J. Crutzen).

The third component of the figure, the hydrological cycle, includes the processes of evaporation and precipitation, runoff and circulation. Water is a key agent of topographic change and an overall regulator of global chemistry and climate. As described by J. W. Maurits la Rivière in Chapter 4, "Threats to the World's Water," human impacts on the hydrological cycle that require attention include pollution of groundwater, surface waters and oceans, redistribution of water flows on the earth's surface and potential sea-level changes induced by global warming.

Life, the final component in Figure 1.3, has found the environment of planet earth to be replete with possibilities, resulting in the evolution of an astounding — but rapidly decreasing — degree of biological diversity (see Chapter 5, "Threats to Biodiversity," by Edward O. Wilson). It has not been widely appreciated until recently that life is also a key player in conditioning and regulating the global environment, through its influence on the chemical and hydrological cycles. Finally, one form of life — the human species — has grown over the past several centuries from a position of negligible influence at the planetary scale to one of great significance as an agent of global change.

Although our knowledge of the earth system is quickly expanding, we do not yet know enough about it to say with any certainty how much change the system as a whole can tolerate or what its capacity may be for sustaining human development. We do, however, know a good deal about interactions between individual components of the global environment and specific human activities. This admittedly incomplete knowledge provides some useful perspectives on questions of planetary management.

Since the beginning of the 18th century, the human population has increased by a factor of eight; average life expectancy has at least doubled. During the same period human economic activity has become increasingly global, with demands for goods and services in one part of the planet being met with supplies from half a world away. The volume of goods exchanged in international trade has increased by a factor of 800 or more and now represents more than a third of the world's total economic product.

The three components of this growth and globalization of human activity that have had greatest impact on the environment are agriculture, energy and manufacturing, each of which is discussed at length in subsequent chapters. Agriculture has been the dominant agent of global land transformation; since the middle of the last century, nine million square kilometers of the earth's surface have been converted into permanent croplands (see Chapter 7, "Strategies for Agriculture," by Pierre R. Crosson and Norman J. Rosenberg). Energy use has risen by a factor of 80 over the same period, with profound consequences for the planet's chemical flows of carbon, sulfur and nitrogen (see Chapter 8 "Strategies for Energy Use," by John H. Gibbons, Peter D. Blair and Holly L. Gwin). Finally, the world's industrial production has increased more than 100-fold in 100 years, supported by long-term growth rates of more than 3 percent a year in the utilization of such basic metals as lead, copper and iron (see Chapter 9, "Strategies for Manufacturing," by Robert A. Frosch and Nicholas E. Gallopoulos).

The transformation of the planetary environment induced by this explosion of human activity is particularly evident in changes to the physical landscape. Since the beginning of the 18th century, the planet has lost six million square kilometers of forest — an area larger than Europe. Land degradation has increased to a significant but uncertain degree (see Figure 1.4). Sediment loads have risen threefold in major river systems and eightfold in smaller basins that support intense human activity; the resulting flow of carbon to the sea is between one and two billion tons a year. During the same period the amount of water humans withdraw from the hydrological cycle has increased from perhaps 100 to 3,600 cubic kilometers per year — a volume equivalent to that of Lake Huron.

Many substantial changes in the planet's other chemical flows have taken place. In the past 300 years agricultural and industrial development has doubled the amount of methane in the atmosphere and increased the concentration of carbon dioxide by 25 percent (see Figure 1.5). The global flows of major elements such as sulfur and nitrogen that result from human activity are comparable to or greater than the natural flows of these elements. Among the trace metals, many of which are toxic to life, Jerome O. Nriagu of the Canadian National Water Research Institute and Jozef M. Pacyna of the

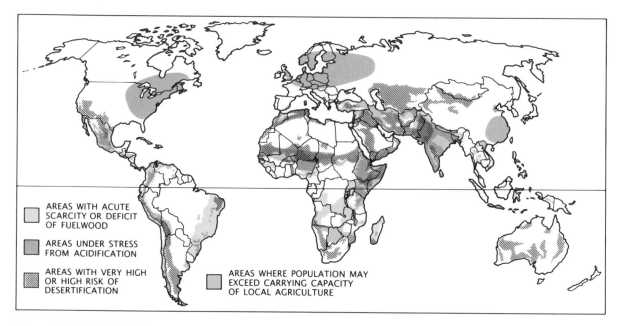

Figure 1.4 LAND DEGRADATION results from a variety of human activities. Shown are regions threatened by desertification, overharvesting of firewood, acid rain and stress induced by efforts to feed more people than the land is actually able to support. The data are from the U.N.'s Food and Agriculture Organization and the Scientific Committee on Problems of the Environment.

Norwegian Institute for Air Pollution Research have shown that human emissions of lead, cadmium and zinc exceed the flux from natural sources by factors of 18, five and three, respectively. For several other metals, including arsenic, mercury, nickel and vanadium, the human contribution is now as much as two times that from natural sources. Finally, of the more than 70,000 chemicals synthesized by humans, a number—such as the chlorofluorocarbons and DDT—have been shown to affect the global environment significantly, even at very low concentrations.

Assessment of the prospects for sustainable development of the earth shows that the change in the rates at which human activities are transforming the planet may be as important as the absolute magnitudes involved. B. L. Turner, Robert W. Kates and I have analyzed historical transformation rates for several components of the global environmental system. For each component, we first characterized the recency of change—the date by which half of the total human transformation from prehistoric times to the present had taken place. Next, we assessed the acceleration of change by comparing the present rate of transformation with that of a generation ago. The dominant impression from this analysis is the relative recency of most global environmental change. None of the components we reviewed had reached 50 percent of its total transformation before the 19th century. Most passed the 50 percent level only in the second half of the 20th century.

Beyond this general conclusion, four broad patterns of transformation emerge. The first pattern, characterized by relatively long-established and still accelerating change, includes deforestation and soil erosion. The second, established relatively recently and still accelerating, includes the destruction of floral diversity, withdrawal of water from the hydrological cycle, sediment flows and human mobilization of carbon, nitrogen and phosphorus. There is little reason to believe that human society has yet learned to manage on a global scale any of these accelerating transformations of the environment.

More encouraging are two decelerating trends. Human-induced extinctions of terrestrial vertebrates reached half of their present total by the late

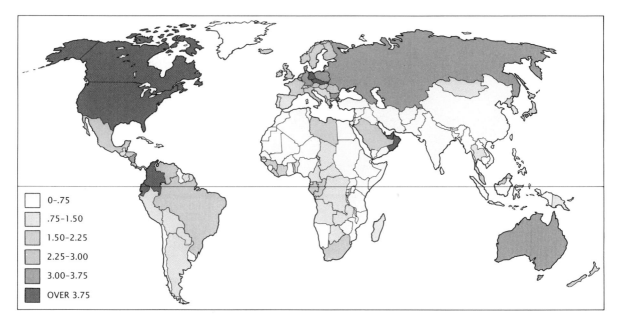

Figure 1.5 CARBON DIOXIDE EMISSIONS are one impact of human activities on the environment. Shown are carbon dioxide releases from energy use, industrial activities and deforestation expressed as tons of carbon per person per year. Highest are East Germany and the U.S. Lowest are Burundi and Bhutan. Data were compiled by the author's student Susan Subak.

19th century and are apparently occurring more slowly today than they were a generation ago. The remaining group of transformations we examined —releases of sulfur, lead, radioactive fallout, a representative organic solvent and extinction of marine mammals—also represents primarily phenomena of the 20th century that are now decelerating.

The crude measure of long-term deceleration presented here gives no assurance that the declining transformation rates reflect increasing competence in planetary management. (Specific transformation rates could, for example, decline simply because there are no more species to exterminate or because we turn to cheaper fuels that happen to emit different pollutants.) Nevertheless, for most of the cases I have cited, at least some fraction of the deceleration can be attributed to deliberate large-scale, long-term efforts at environmental management.

The global patterns sketched so far provide a necessary but insufficient perspective from which to reflect on the prospects for improving the management of planet earth. Also needed is an appreciation of the regional faces of change. To ana-lyze regional situations in any detail is beyond the scope of this essay; still, it will be helpful to recall the extraordinary range of local circumstances that will have to be dealt with if the human transformation of the planet is to be steered along paths of sustainable development.

Any classification of regional perspectives on sustainable development will inevitably oversimplify reality. But one of the most instructive simplifications distinguishes interactions between environment and development that are associated with poverty from those associated with affluence. Another distinguishes interactions involving low population densities from those with high population densities. Combining the two simplifications yields the classification shown in Figure 1.6.

Low-income, low-density areas such as Amazonia and Malaya-Borneo constitute settlement frontiers still available for use by people in the less developed countries. Until recently, such regions supported sparse populations, and intrusions from the industrialized world were confined to small plantation and mining sites. The situation has changed dramatically during the past 20 years as

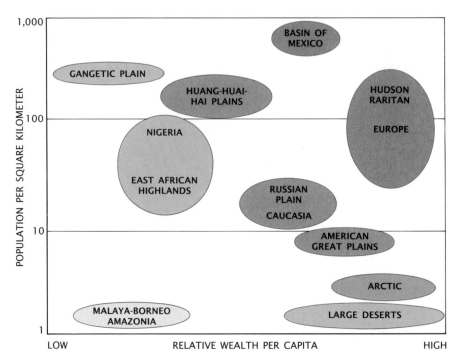

Figure 1.6 REGIONAL VARIETIES of environmental transformation can be visualized by plotting population density versus relative wealth. Regions with low density and low industrialization include many of the earth's remaining settlement frontiers. Low-density areas with relatively high investments tend to be the harsh environments exploited by corporate developers of fuel and minerals. High-density, low-income regions have long histories of agricultural development. The greatest responsibility for designing sustainable-development strategies lies with the high-density, wealthy regions that have imposed a disproportionate burden on the planet's environment. The figure is from work by B. L. Turner, Robert W. Kates and the author.

humans engaged in large-scale timber clearing and livestock raising have invaded these regions. The resulting mix of subsistence and commercial agriculture plus industrial resource extraction has led to a unique pattern of landscape transformation, the full implications of which cannot yet be assessed. Reduction of biological diversity and degradation of biological productivity nonetheless seem inevitable (see Chapter 5, "Threats to Biodiversity," by Edward O. Wilson). The poverty of the landless farmers engaged in land clearing and the relative paucity of indigenous institutions that might guide the sustainable development of such regions will make them especially problematic components of any strategy for planetary management.

In contrast, regions with low population density but high investments in sophisticated technology are illustrated by the classic harsh environments of the earth. Such environments include the circumpolar arctic areas, deserts, mineral-extraction platforms and off-shore "fish factories." The large-scale transformation of these regions has become possible only within the past several decades as knowledge, prices and technology have converged to induce development.

Of the environmental changes associated with such development — oil spills, river diversions and landscape transformation — some have received widespread attention. Others, such as atmospheric pollution and cultural dislocation, have received less. The knowledge base for management remains poor. But since a relatively few, wealthy corporate actors seem likely to be involved in most transformations of consequence, the possibilities for institutionalizing sustainable-development strategies for such regions may be relatively good.

Typical of low-income, high-density regions are the Gangetic Plain of the Indian subcontinent and the Huang-Huai-Hai Plains of China. Here intensive agricultural development has been under way for centuries and has been joined in the past several decades by the rapid rise of industrial development in growing urban centers. Landscape degradation is the central problem as more and more people are employed on agricultural land that is already exploited to capacity (see Figure 1.7). In addition, the rapid rise of heavy industry in such areas has led to pollution problems comparable to those that Europe faced several decades ago. The critical management challenge here is to provide employment that generates income and takes pressure off the land without aggravating urbanization problems or increasing regional competition for "smokestack" industries.

The greatest responsibility and the greatest immediate potential for the design of sustainable-development strategies may be in the high-income, high-density regions of the industrialized world. As is repeatedly stated in discussions of stratospheric ozone depletion and the greenhouse effect, advanced industrialized societies have been responsible for imposing a disproportionate share of global environmental burdens on the planet. Over the past several decades, however, places as different as Sweden, Japan and the northeastern U.S. have all achieved significant improvement in numerous aspects of their regional environments. Forests have expanded, sulfur emissions have declined, locally extinct species have been successfully reintroduced. Some of these environmental victories are clearly the unintended by-product of unrelated economic changes. Others reflect the export of environmentally destructive activities to less fortunate parts of the world. Increasingly, however, such regions are benefiting from systematic strategies to mitigate the impacts of uncontrolled development and are beginning to design the kinds of environments in which their people want to live.

What kind of environments can such strategies attain? What kinds of development can they sustain? Apart from a basic knowledge of how the global environment works and how human development interacts with it, an understanding is also required of the impact that policy can have on environmental change.

At the outset, it cannot be overemphasized that policy for managing planet earth must above all else be adaptive (see Chapter 11, "Toward a Sustainable World," by William D. Ruckelshaus). Our understanding of the science behind global change is incomplete and will remain so into the foreseeable future. Surprises like the stratospheric ozone hole will continue to appear and will demand action well in advance of scientific certainty. Our understanding of the economic and social processes that contribute to global environmental change is even weaker. Conventional forecasts of population and energy growth could turn out to be conventional foolishness. Science can help, but it is our capacity to shape adaptive policies able to cope with surprises that will determine our effectiveness as managers of planet earth. Building such a capacity will require cultivation of leadership and of institutional competence in at least four areas.

The first requirement is to make the information on which individuals and institutions base their decisions more supportive of sustainable-development objectives. Part of the task, it cannot be said often enough, is simply to support the basic scientific research and planetary monitoring activities that underlie our knowledge of global change. Also essential is to improve the flow of information implicit in existing systems of prices, regulations and economic incentives. The failure of current economic accounts to track the real environmental costs of human activities encourages the inefficient use of resources. The artificially high prices maintained for many agricultural products have significantly exacerbated problems of land degradation and pollution in many parts of the world. Narrowly targeted government subsidies have been directly responsible for a significant fraction of today's global deforestation. All of these distorted information signals need to be addressed in designing adaptive policies for sustainable development.

A second requirement for adaptive planetary management is the invention and implementation of technologies for sustainable development. Such technologies will need to be resource-conserving, pollution-preventing or environment-restoring and at the same time economically sustainable. The chapters on agriculture, energy and manufacturing in this book show that significant technical progress has already been made toward delivering desired end-use services at significantly lower environmental costs. Surprisingly often, the economic costs of the "conserving technologies" also turn out to be lower: cost advantages—not environmental concerns—are responsible for halving the ratio of energy consumption to the gross national product in the U.S. since it peaked in the early 1920's.

Technologies for the restoration of environments

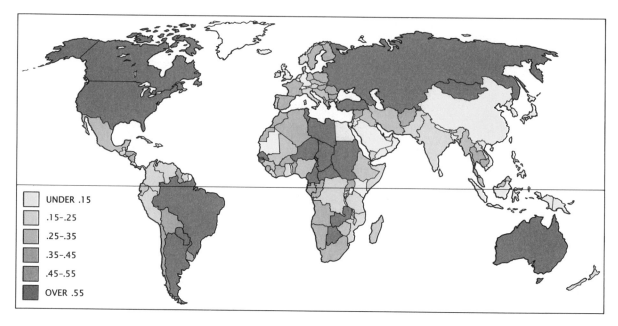

Figure 1.7 CROPLAND PER CAPITA is an index of the flexibility societies have to adjust their land-use practices. Shown here is cropland in hectares per capita for the mid-1980's. Countries with less than about .2 hectare per capita are especially limited in their options for managing the environment. Data are from the United Nations Food and Agriculture Organization.

degraded by salinization, acidification and mining have also been developed and are being effectively employed on a regional scale. The policy need is to tailor technological innovations to the specific local conditions encountered in various environment-development conflicts around the world.

A third requirement for adaptive planetary management is the construction of mechanisms at the national and international level to coordinate managerial activities. The need for formal international agreements in this area has been highlighted by the Montreal Protocol on Substances that Deplete the Ozone Layer and discussion of a possible international law of the atmosphere. In fact, a dozen or more global conventions for protection of the environment are now in effect.

Beneath this orderly surface, however, a large and rapidly growing number of nongovernmental bodies, governmental agencies and international organizations are scrambling to play some part in the management of planet earth. Pluralism has much to recommend it. But are we not nearing a point of diminishing returns where too many meetings, too many declarations and too many visiting experts leave too few people with too few resources and too little time to actually do anything? The immediate need at the international level is for a forum in which ministerial-level coordination of environmental-management activities can be regularly discussed and implemented, much as is already done for international economic policy. As in the case of economic policy, the existence of such a formal, high-level governmental summit on global issues of environment and development could provide an occasion for parallel discussions involving nongovernmental and private-sector interests.

Finally, building a capacity for adaptive management of planet earth will require a desire and an ability to reflect continually on the values and objectives that guide our efforts. In an important sense, there has turned out to be more to the notion of sustainable development than even the wise members of the World Commission intended. Individuals, organizations and entire nations have taken the concept as a point of departure for rethinking their interactions with the global environment.

In the Soviet Union, issues of ecological deterioration became a central point of debate in the first

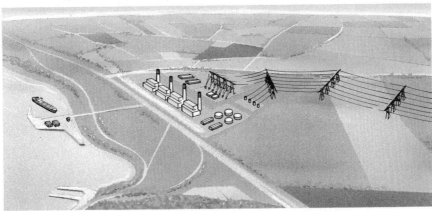

Figure 1.8 "PAINTING THE FUTURE" is the title of a Swedish study in which environmentalist Lars Emmelin and artist Gunnar Brusewitz collaborated to paint the Swedish landscape as it might appear under various paths of development. In these paintings, the Dybäck region of southern Sweden is shown as it might look in 2015. At the top is the area in a "Solar Sweden" scenario of wind power and biomass plantations; at the bottom is one vision of the "Nuclear Sweden" scenario.

Congress of People's Deputies. In Kenya, an innovative project sponsored by the African Academy of Sciences has begun to explore and articulate alternative possibilities for the continent's development in the 21st century. In West Germany, a high-level commission representing all political parties and the scientific community evolved a consensual *Vorsorge*, or prevention, principle to guide the nation's environmental policies. In Sweden, a national best-seller and focal point for political debate emerged when environmental scientists and artist Gunnar Bruse-witz collaborated in "painting the future" of Swedish landscapes under alternative paths of development (see Figure 1.8).

The impact that these and similar explorations being conducted around the world will ultimately have in guiding the human transformation of the environment is far from clear. But there can be no question that, against all expectations, the explorations all reflect an emerging commitment to get on with the task of managing planet earth in a responsible manner.

The Changing Atmosphere

Human activity is altering the complex mixture of gases in the atmosphere. Some effects, such as acid rain and smog, are already evident. Unwelcome surprises may be lurking.

. . .

Thomas E. Graedel and Paul J. Crutzen

The earth's atmosphere has never been free of change: its composition, temperature and self-cleansing ability have all varied since the planet first formed. Yet the pace in the past two centuries has been remarkable: the atmosphere's composition in particular has changed significantly faster than it has at any time in human history.

The increasingly evident effects of the ongoing changes include acid deposition by rain and other processes, corrosion of materials, urban smog and a thinning of the stratospheric ozone (O_3) shield that protects the earth from harmful ultraviolet radiation. Atmospheric scientists expect also that the planet will soon warm rapidly (causing potentially dramatic climatic shifts) through enhancement of the greenhouse effect—the heating of the earth by gases that absorb infrared radiation from the sun-warmed surface of the planet and then return the radiation to the earth.

Surprisingly, these important phenomena do not stem from modifications in the atmosphere's major constituents. Excluding the widely varying content of water vapor, the concentrations of the gases that make up more than 99.9 percent of the atmosphere—nitrogen (N_2), oxygen (O_2) and totally unreactive noble gases—have been nearly constant for much longer than human beings have been on the earth. Rather, the effects are caused in large part by changes, mainly increases, in the levels of several of the atmosphere's minor constituents, or trace gases. Such gases include sulfur dioxide (SO_2), two nitrogen oxides known collectively as NO_x—nitric oxide (NO) and nitrogen dioxide (NO_2)—and several chlorofluorocarbons (compounds that contain chlorine, fluorine, carbon and sometimes hydrogen).

Sulfur dioxide, for example, rarely constitutes as much as 50 parts per billion of the atmosphere, even where its emissions are highest, and yet it contributes to acid deposition, to the corrosion of

Figure 2.1 BURNING OF VEGETATION, a common practice in the tropics, releases soot and several gases, particularly carbon dioxide (CO_2), carbon monoxide (CO), hydrocarbons, nitric oxide (NO) and nitrogen dioxide (NO_2). This and other human activities—such as the burning of fossil fuels—account to a great extent for dramatic increases over the past two centuries in the atmospheric concentrations of many trace gases. These increases are giving rise to such environmental perturbations as acid deposition, urban smog and depletion of the stratospheric ozone layer that absorbs damaging ultraviolet radiation. Warming of the planet is also expected, from the buildup of greenhouse gases that trap infrared radiation.

stone and metal and to the aesthetic nuisance of decreased visibility. The NO_x compounds, which are similarly scarce, are important in the formation of both acid deposition and what is called photochemical smog, a product of solar-driven chemical reactions in the atmosphere. The chlorofluorocarbons, which as a group account for just one part per billion or so of the atmosphere, are the agents primarily responsible for depleting the stratospheric ozone layer. In addition, rising levels of chlorofluorocarbons, together with methane (CH_4), nitrous oxide (N_2O) and carbon dioxide (CO_2)—by far the most abundant trace gas at 350 parts per million—are enhancing the greenhouse effect.

The hydroxyl radical (OH), a highly reactive molecular fragment, also influences atmospheric activity even though it is much scarcer than the other gases, with a concentration of less than .00001 part per billion. Hydroxyl plays a different role, however: it contributes to the cleansing of the atmosphere. Its abundance in the atmosphere may diminish in the future.

Certainly some fluctuation in the concentrations of atmospheric constituents can derive from variations in rates of emission by natural sources. Volcanoes, for instance, can release sulfur- and chlorine-containing gases into the troposphere (the lower 10 to 15 kilometers of the atmosphere) and the stratosphere (extending roughly from 10 to 50 kilometers above the surface). The fact remains, however, that the activities of human beings account for most of the rapid changes of the past 200 years. Such activities include the combustion of fossil fuels (coal and petroleum) for energy, other industrial and agricultural practices, biomass burning (the burning of vegetation) and deforestation.

So much is clear, but which human activities generate which emissions? How do altered concentrations of trace gases give rise to such an array of effects? How much have the problems grown, and what are their consequences for the planet? Although complete answers to these questions are still forthcoming, multidisciplinary efforts by chemists, meteorologists, solar and space physicists, geophysicists, biologists, ecologists and others are making good headway.

Multidisciplinary collaboration is crucial because the factors influencing the fates of the gases in the atmosphere and their interactions with the biosphere are complex and incompletely understood. For instance, the chemical reactions a gas undergoes in the atmosphere can vary depending on the local mixture of gases and particles, the temperature, the intensity of the sun, the presence of different kinds of clouds or precipitation and patterns of airflow (which move chemicals horizontally and vertically). The reactions, in turn, influence how long a gas remains in the atmosphere and hence whether the gas or its end products have global or more localized effects on the environment (see Figure 2.2).

Among the fruits of the investigations has been an improved understanding of the emissions produced by specific human activities. The combustion of fossil fuels for energy is known to yield substantial amounts of sulfur dioxide (particularly from coal), nitrogen oxides (which form when nitrogen and oxygen in the air are heated) and carbon dioxide. If the burning is incomplete, it also yields carbon monoxide (CO), a variety of hydrocarbons (including methane) and soot (carbon particles). Other industrial activities release additional sulfur dioxide (smelting is an example) or inject such substances as chlorofluorocarbons or toxic metals into the air.

Agricultural practices lead to the emissions of several gases as well. The burning of forests and savanna grasses in tropical and subtropical regions to create pastures and cropland yields additional large amounts of carbon monoxide, methane and nitrogen oxides (see Figure 2.1). Moreover, soil exposed after forests are cleared emits nitrous oxide, as do nitrogen-rich fertilizers spread over fields. The breeding of domestic animals is another major source of methane (from oxygen-shunning bacteria in the digestive tract of cattle and other cud-chewing animals), as is the cultivation of rice, which is a staple food for many people in the tropics and subtropics.

Recent investigations have also led to a better understanding of the effects produced by increased anthropogenic emissions. For example, the much studied phenomenon of "acid rain" (by which we mean also acid snow, fog and dew) is now known to develop mainly as a by-product of atmospheric interactions involving the NO_x gases and sulfur dioxide. Through various reactions, such as combination with the hydroxyl radical, these gases can be converted within days into nitric acid (HNO_3) and sulfuric acid (H_2SO_4), both of which are dissolved readily in water. When the acidified droplets fall to the earth's surface, they constitute acid rain.

Because water droplets are removed from the atmosphere rapidly, acid rain is a regional or continental, rather than global, phenomenon. In con-

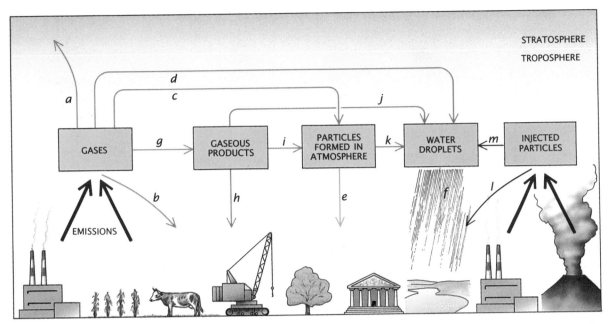

Figure 2.2 FATE OF EMISSIONS can vary. A gas (*orange arrows*) that is unreactive and insoluble in water (*a*) will spread through the troposphere and in some cases into the stratosphere, although a fraction may be taken up by land and water surfaces (*b*). A soluble gas may dissolve in moisture on particles (*c*) or in water droplets (*d*), which carry the gas to the earth (*green arrows*) directly (*e*) or in rain, snow, fog or dew (*f*). Most gases undergo chemical changes in the atmosphere (*g*), and resulting gaseous products (*purple arrows*) can sometimes be deposited dry on the earth (*h*), but they are also more readily incorporated into wetted particles (*i*) and, directly (*j*) or indirectly (*k*), into water droplets. The fate of injected particles (*right*) is similar to that of gases. They can be deposited directly (*l*) or else incorporated into water (*m*) and returned to the earth in precipitation (*f*).

trast, the atmospheric lifetimes of several other trace gases, including methane, carbon dioxide, the chlorofluorocarbons and nitrous oxide, are much longer (see Figure 2.3), and so the gases spread rather evenly throughout the atmosphere, causing global effects.

Since the beginning of the Industrial Revolution in the mid-18th century, the acidity of precipitation (as measured by the concentration of hydrogen ions) has increased in many places. For example, it has roughly quadrupled in the northeastern U.S. since 1900, paralleling increased emissions of sulfur dioxide and the NO_x gases. Similar increases have been found elsewhere in the industrialized parts of the world. Acid rain has also been detected in the virtually unindustrialized tropics, where it stems mainly from the release of the NO_x gases and hydrocarbons by biomass burning.

Wet deposition is not the only way sulfuric and nitric acids in the troposphere find their way to the earth's surface. The acids can also be deposited "dry," as gases or as constituents of microscopic particles. Indeed, a growing body of evidence indicates that dry deposition can cause the same environmental problems as the wet form.

Acid deposition clearly places severe stress on many ecosystems. Although the specific interactions of such deposition with lake fauna, soils and different vegetation types are still incompletely understood, acid deposition is known to have strongly increased the acidity of lakes in Scandinavia, the northeastern U.S. and southeastern Canada, thereby leading to reductions in the size and diversity of fish populations. Such deposition also appears to play some role in the forest damage that has been discovered in parts of the northeastern U.S. and Europe.

There is little doubt that acids deposited from the troposphere also contribute to the corrosion of outdoor equipment, buildings and works of art, partic-

GAS	GREENHOUSE EFFECT	STRATOSPHERIC OZONE DEPLETION	ACID DEPOSITION	SMOG	CORROSION	DECREASED VISIBILITY	DECREASED SELF-CLEANSING OF ATMOSPHERE
CARBON MONOXIDE (CO)							+
CARBON DIOXIDE (CO_2)	+	+/−					
METHANE (CH_4)	+	+/−					+/−
NO_x: NITRIC OXIDE (NO) AND NITROGEN DIOXIDE (NO_2)		+/−	+	+		+	−
NITROUS OXIDE (N_2O)	+	+/−					
SULFUR DIOXIDE (SO_2)	−		+		+	+	
CHLOROFLUORO-CARBONS	+	+					
OZONE (O_3)	+			+			−

GAS	MAJOR ANTHROPOGENIC SOURCES	ANTHROPOGENIC/TOTAL EMISSIONS PER YEAR (MILLIONS OF TONS)	AVERAGE RESIDENCE TIME IN ATMOSPHERE	AVERAGE CONCENTRATION 100 YEARS AGO (PPB)	APPROXIMATE CURRENT CONCENTRATION (PPB)	PROJECTED CONCENTRATION IN YEAR 2030 (PPB)
CARBON MONOXIDE (CO)	Fossil-Fuel Combustion, Biomass Burning	700/2,000	Months	?, N. Hem. 40 to 80, S. Hem. (Clean Atmospheres)	100 to 200, N. Hem. 40 to 80, S. Hem. (Clean Atmospheres)	Probably Increasing
CARBON DIOXIDE (CO_2)	Fossil-Fuel Combustion, Deforestation	5,500/~5,500	100 Years	290,000	350,000	400,000 to 550,000
METHANE (CH_4)	Rice Fields, Cattle, Landfills, Fossil-Fuel Production	300 to 400/550	10 Years	900	1,700	2,200 to 2,500
NO_x GASES	Fossil-Fuel Combustion, Biomass Burning	20 to 30/ 30 to 50	Days	.001 to ? (Clean to Industrial)	.001 to 50 Clean to Industrial)	.001 to 50 (Clean to Industrial)
NITROUS OXIDE (N_2O)	Nitrogenous Fertilizers, Deforestation, Biomass Burning	6/25	170 Years	285	310	330 to 350
SULFUR DIOXIDE (SO_2)	Fossil-Fuel Combustion, Ore Smelting	100 to 130/ 150 to 200	Days To Weeks	.03 to ? (Clean to Industrial)	.03 to 50 (Clean to Industrial)	.03 to 50 (Clean to Industrial)
CHLOROFLUORO-CARBONS	Aerosol Sprays, Refrigerants, Foams	~1/1	60 to 100 Years	0	About 3 (Chlorine atoms)	2.4 to 6 (Chlorine atoms)

Figure 2.3 TRACE GASES and the environmental perturbations with which they are associated are listed (*top*). Plus signs indicate a contribution to the effect; minus signs indicate amelioration. Sometimes a gas's effect varies, indicated by dual signs (+/−). The concentrations of many gases, given in parts per billion (ppb), are expected to be significantly higher 40 years from now (*bottom*) if anthropogenic emissions continue to increase. The concentrations of the NO_x gases and sulfur dioxide over highly industrial sites may not rise much in 40 years, but the number of polluted sites can be expected to grow, particularly in the developing nations. Chlorofluorocarbon concentrations are given in terms of chlorine atoms.

ularly in urban areas—costing tens of billions of dollars each year for repairs and equipment replacement in the U.S. alone. Particles containing sulfate (SO_4^{2-}) have other effects as well. By scattering light efficiently, they decrease visibility; by influencing cloud albedo, they may have important implications for climate (see Chapter 3, "The Changing Climate," by Stephen H. Schneider).

In and around cities photochemical smog is another negative consequence of modern life (see Figure 2.4). The term technically refers to the undesirable mixture of gases formed in the lower troposphere when solar radiation acts on anthropogenic emissions (particularly the NO_x gases and hydrocarbons from vehicle exhaust) to produce reactive gases that can be destructive to living organisms.

Ozone is a major product of such photochemical reactions and is itself the main cause of smog-induced eye irritation, impaired lung function and damage to trees and crops. The severity of smog is therefore generally assessed on the basis of ground-level ozone concentrations. In other words, the same three-oxygen molecule that is critically important for absorbing ultraviolet radiation in the stratosphere, where some 90 percent of atmospheric ozone is concentrated, is a problem when it accumulates in excess near the earth's surface.

Investigators have measured ozone levels in the atmosphere since the late 19th century, first from the ground and then within the atmosphere, aided by sophisticated airborne devices. Some of the earliest data showed that the "natural" level of ozone close to the ground at one measuring post in Europe roughly a century ago was about 10 parts per billion. Today the typical ground-level concentrations in Western Europe are from two to four times higher. Abundances more than 10 times higher than the natural level are now often recorded in Western Europe, California, the eastern U.S. and Australia.

Photochemical smog is also appearing in broad regions of the tropics and subtropics, particularly because of the periodic burning of savanna grasses; the same territories may be set afire as often as once a year. This practice releases large amounts of precursors to smog. Because solar radiation is plentiful and strong in those regions and photochemical reactions occur quickly, ozone levels can readily climb to perhaps five times higher than normal. As the populations in the tropics and subtropics grow, unhealthy air should become even more widespread there. Such a prospect is particularly worrisome be-

cause the properties of the soil in those regions may make the ecosystems there more vulnerable than the ecosystems in the middle latitudes to smog's effects.

Although a decrease in ozone near the ground would benefit polluted regions, any decrease in stratospheric ozone is disturbing, because the resulting increase in ultraviolet radiation reaching the earth could have many serious effects. It could elevate the incidence of skin cancer and cataracts in human beings, and it might damage crops and phytoplankton, the microscopic plants that are the basis of the food chain in the ocean.

So far, the extent of stratospheric ozone depletion has been most dramatic over Antarctica, where an ozone "hole," a region of increasingly severe ozone loss, has appeared each southern spring since about 1975. In the past decade springtime ozone levels over Antarctica have diminished by about 50 percent [see "The Antarctic Ozone Hole," by Richard S. Stolarski; SCIENTIFIC AMERICAN, January, 1988]. A more global assessment of the stratospheric ozone layer is still in a preliminary stage, but in the past 20 years depletions of from 2 to 10 percent have apparently begun to occur during the winter and early spring in the middle-to-high latitudes of the Northern Hemisphere, with the greatest declines in the higher latitudes.

It is now quite evident that chlorofluorocarbons, particularly CFC-11 ($CFCl_3$) and CFC-12 (CF_2Cl_2), are the major culprits responsible for ozone depletion. These anthropogenic chemicals, whose emissions and atmospheric concentrations have grown rapidly since their introduction several decades ago, are widespread as refrigerants, aerosol propellants, solvents and blowing agents for foam production, in part because they have what initially seemed to be a wonderful property: they are virtually unreactive in the lower atmosphere, and so they pose no direct toxic threat to living organisms.

Unfortunately, the very same characteristics that render chlorofluorocarbons rather inert enable them to reach the stratosphere unchanged. There they are exposed to strong ultraviolet radiation, which breaks them apart and liberates chlorine atoms that can destroy ozone by catalyzing its conversion to molecular oxygen. (Catalysts accelerate chemical reactions but are freed unaltered at the end.) Indeed, every chlorine atom ultimately eliminates many thousands of ozone molecules. Primarily because of the emission of chlorofluorocarbons, the level of

Figure 2.4 PHOTOCHEMICAL SMOG, here shrouding São Paulo, Brazil, is a problem in many urban areas. It forms when solar radiation acts on emissions — notably nitrogen oxides and hydrocarbons from vehicle exhaust — to produce an undesirable mixture of gases near the ground. The major component is ozone, which can harm the eyes and lungs and damage trees and crops.

ozone-destroying chlorinated compounds in the stratosphere is now four to five times higher than normal and is increasing at a rate of approximately 5 percent a year — developments that highlight the profound effect human activity can have on the stratosphere.

Stratospheric ozone (O_3) is formed initially when an oxygen molecule (O_2) absorbs shortwave radiation, which splits it into two oxygen atoms (O); each atom then combines with another oxygen molecule to form ozone. Usually, photochemical reactions catalyzed by the NO_x gases remove ozone at a rate equal to the rate of its formation. Chlorine catalytic cycles, which are growing rapidly in importance in the atmosphere, disturb this natural balance and result in a net ozone loss (see box, "Chemical Reactions in the Atmosphere," on page 19).

Particularly in Antarctica and to a lesser extent in the Arctic, frigid temperatures hasten the chlorine-catalytic cycles by removing nitrogen oxides, which strongly interfere with them. (Paradoxically, then, although the NO_x gases can destroy ozone, their presence in the stratosphere often ameliorates chlorine-catalyzed ozone destruction.) Together with water molecules, the NO_x gases freeze to form particles making up what are known as polar strato-

---

CHEMICAL REACTIONS IN THE ATMOSPHERE

OXIDIZERS AS DETERGENTS. The molecular species that initiate most atmospheric reactions ("oxidizers" in the chemist's terminology) can be regarded as detergents because they transform gases into water-soluble products, thereby facilitating their removal in precipitation. Ozone (O_3) is one important oxidizer and also participates in the formation of another detergent: the hydroxyl radical (OH), which interacts with nearly every molecular species in the atmosphere. Much of the trace gases that have been emitted into the atmosphere would still be there were it nor for these substances. The hydroxyl radical forms after ultraviolet light (hv) dissociates ozone, releasing a highly energetic—and hence highly reactive—oxygen atom ($O^{\bullet}$) that then combines with a water molecule:

$$\text{a) } O_3 \xrightarrow{hv} O^{\bullet} + O_2 \qquad\qquad \text{b) } O^{\bullet} + H_2O \longrightarrow 2\,OH$$

STRATOSPHERIC OZONE: GENERATION AND LOSS. Ozone forms when oxygen molecules (O_2 are dissociated by ultraviolet radiation and the resulting oxygen atoms combine with other oxygen molecules:

$$\text{a) } O_2 \xrightarrow{hv} O + O \qquad\qquad \text{b) } O + O_2 \longrightarrow O_3$$

Chlorine atoms from chlorofluorocarbon compounds released into the atmosphere play a central role in one of the most efficient ozone-destroying catalytic cycles in the stratosphere. The cycle begins with the breakup of an ozone molecule by atomic chlorine and the formation of chlorine monoxide (ClO) and molecular oxygen:

$$\text{a) } Cl + O_3 \longrightarrow ClO + O_2$$

Then the chlorine monoxide reacts with an oxygen atom (formed by the photodissociation of another ozone molecule) and liberates the chlorine, which can initiate the cycle again:

$$\text{b) } ClO + O \longrightarrow Cl + O_2$$

Nitrogen oxides destroy ozone as well, but they can also interfere with this cycle. For example, nitrogen dioxide can remove chlorine monoxide from circulation by combining with it to form chlorine nitrate ($ClNO_3$).

---

spheric clouds. Worse yet, the cloud particles actually facilitate chemical reactions that release chlorine from compounds that do not themselves react with ozone, such as hydrochloric acid (HCl) and chlorine nitrate ($ClNO_3$).

Even if chlorofluorocarbon emissions stopped today, chemical reactions causing the destruction of stratospheric ozone would continue for at least a century. The reason is simple: the compounds remain that long in the atmosphere and would continue to diffuse into the stratosphere from the tropospheric reservoir long after emissions had ceased.

The depletion of global stratospheric ozone seems to be the handiwork primarily of a single class of industrial products—the chlorofluorocarbons—but several different emissions combine to raise the specter of a rapid greenhouse warming of the earth. Exactly how high global temperatures might climb in the years ahead is not yet clear. What is clear is that the levels of such infrared-absorbing trace gases as carbon dioxide, methane, the chlorofluorocarbons and nitrous oxide have mounted dramatically in the past decades, making added heating inevitable.

The trapping of heat near the surface of the planet by naturally emitted trace gases is a vital process: without it the planet would be too cold for habitation. Yet the prospect of a sudden temperature increase of even a few degrees Celsius is disquieting because no one can accurately predict its environmental effects, such as what the precise changes will be in precipitation around the world and in sea level. Any effects will probably be rapid, however, making it extremely difficult or impossible for the world's ecosystems and for human societies to adapt.

The extraordinary pace of the recent increases in greenhouse gases becomes strikingly evident when modern levels are compared with those of the distant past. Such comparisons have been made for several gases, including carbon dioxide—which alone accounts for more than half of the heat trapped by trace species—and methane, which is a more efficient infrared absorber than carbon dioxide but is significantly less abundant.

The histories of carbon dioxide and methane can be reconstructed on the basis of their concentrations in bubbles of air trapped in ice in such perpetually cold places as Antarctica and Greenland (see Figure 2.5). Because the gases are long-lived and hence are spread fairly evenly throughout the atmosphere, the polar samples reveal the approximate global average concentrations of previous eras.

Analyses of the bubbles in ice samples indicate that carbon dioxide and methane concentrations held steady from the end of the last ice age some 10,000 years ago until roughly 300 years ago, at close to 260 parts per million and 700 parts per billion, respectively. Some 300 years ago the methane levels began to climb, and roughly 100 years ago the levels of both gases began to soar to their current levels of 350 parts per million for carbon dioxide and 1,700 parts per billion for methane. Moreover, direct worldwide measurements made by several investigators during the past decade have shown that atmospheric methane levels are growing more rapidly than those of carbon dioxide, at the remarkably high rate of about 1 percent a year.

The increases of both gases in the 20th century must be attributed in large part to the many expanding human influences on emissions. For carbon dioxide the sources are mainly fossil-fuel combustion and deforestation in the tropics; for methane, mainly rice cultivation, cattle breeding, biomass burning in tropical forests and savannas, microbial activity in municipal landfills and leakage of gas during the recovery and distribution of coal, oil and natural gas. As the world's population grows during the next century—and with it the demand for more energy, rice and meat products—the atmospheric concentration of methane could double. The climatic warming caused by methane and other trace gases could well approach that caused by carbon dioxide.

What are the expected trends for other trace gases? We as well as several other workers have extrapolated from the past and the present to make projections for the future, taking into account such factors as estimated increases both in population and in energy consumption. The estimates indicate that increases can be expected in the atmospheric concentrations of virtually all trace species in the next 100 years if new technologies and major energy-conservation efforts are not instituted to diminish the expected dependence on high-sulfur coal, an environmentally disadvantageous fuel, as the world's major energy source.

For example, as part of a multicenter collaboration, we have looked at past sulfur dioxide concentrations over the eastern U.S. and Europe (estimated prior to the mid-1960's on the basis of emission rates) and have speculated about future levels there and over the little-industrialized Gangetic Plain of India (see Figure 2.6). The historical assessment for the U.S. shows a marked increase in sulfur dioxide concentrations between 1890 and 1940, paralleling the buildup of "smokestack" industries and the construction of many new power plants. The amount of sulfur dioxide then leveled off and decreased in the 1960's and early 1970's. To a great extent, the decrease reflects the increased exploitation of oil (which is low in sulfur) for energy as well as the success of clean-air legislation in curbing sulfur emissions.

The concentrations of sulfur dioxide increased over Europe between 1890 and the mid-1900's but then leveled off; they did not decline appreciably, because until recently emission-control efforts were less vigorous than in the U.S. For the Gangetic Plain, where industrialization is rather recent, sulfur dioxide concentrations over some places have climbed from almost nothing in 1890 to levels that are now approaching those over the northeastern U.S.

The average sulfur dioxide concentrations over all three large regions are expected to increase, in part because low-sulfur fuels will probably become scarcer (although extremely stringent emission controls could stabilize levels over the U.S. and Europe for a few decades). The increases could be most marked over India and other developing countries that have rapidly growing populations and access to abundant supplies of high-sulfur coal, which is relatively inexpensive. Clearly, major measures must be introduced in the energy sector to prevent

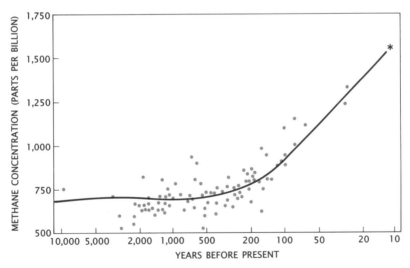

Figure 2.5 CRYSTALS OF ICE in a sample taken from the Greenland ice sheet are about 1,000 years old. The very small air bubbles that are visible hold clues to the ancient concentrations of trace gases. Studies of ice cores from Greenland and Antarctica indicate that the average global concentration of methane held steady near 700 ppb between 10,000 and 300 years ago and then began a dramatic climb about 100 years ago (*bottom*). The red dots represent data from the ice; the asterisk represents the average global value for the late 1970's. (Micrograph by Chester C. Langway, Jr., of the State University of New York at Buffalo.)

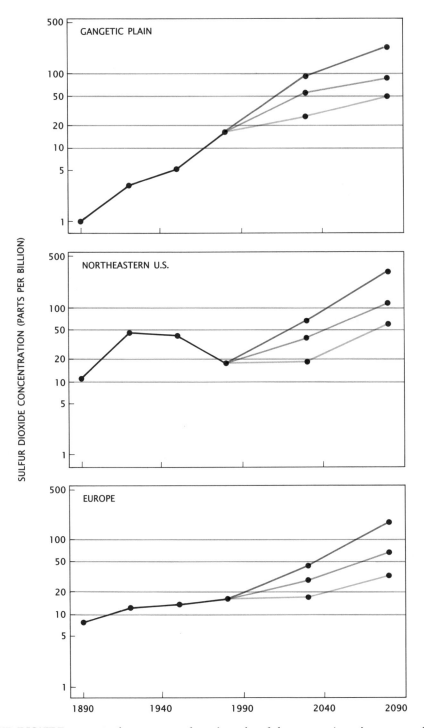

Figure 2.6 SULFUR DIOXIDE concentrations over newly industrializing regions, such as the Gangetic Plain of India, as well as over the northeastern U.S. and Europe have been reviewed (*black*) and projected 100 years ahead (*colors*). The projections assume that each region's population and energy consumption will grow and that the burn-ing of coal for energy (a major source of sulfur dioxide) will increase. The projections differ according to how stringent emission controls might be: mild (*red*), moderate (*orange*) or severe (*green*). The findings indicate that sulfur dioxide levels are likely to increase.

sulfur dioxide concentrations from rising extremely high.

Increases may also occur in a gas we have not yet discussed in detail: carbon monoxide, which has the power to decrease the self-cleansing ability of the atmosphere. A rise in carbon monoxide concentrations is likely because its sources—fossil-fuel combustion, biomass burning and atmospheric reactions involving methane—are all expected to increase. On the other hand, a significant (but still not well-quantified) amount of the gas is formed in the atmosphere over the tropics from the breakdown of hydrocarbons emitted by vegetation, a source that human activities are removing. The future concentrations of carbon monoxide are therefore uncertain, although on balance many workers foresee a rise over the Northern Hemisphere.

Carbon monoxide undermines the self-cleansing ability of the atmosphere by lowering the concentration of the hydroxyl radical, which is an important "detergent" because it reacts with nearly every trace-gas molecule in the atmosphere, including substances that would otherwise be inert. Without hydroxyl, the concentrations of most trace gases would become much higher than those of today, and the atmosphere as a whole would have totally different chemical, physical and climatic properties.

Our projections for the future are discouraging, then, if one assumes that human activities will continue to emit large quantities of undesirable trace gases into the atmosphere. Humanity's unremitting growth and development not only are changing the chemistry of the atmosphere but also are driving the earth rapidly toward a climatic warming of unprecedented magnitude. This climatic change, in combination with increased concentrations of various gases, constitutes a potentially hazardous experiment in which everyone on the earth is taking part.

What is particularly troubling is the possibility of unwelcome surprises, as human activities continue to tax an atmosphere whose inner workings and interactions with organisms and nonliving materials are incompletely understood. The Antarctic ozone hole is a particularly ominous example of the surprises that may be lurking ahead. Its unexpected severity has demonstrated beyond doubt that the atmosphere can be exquisitely sensitive to what seem to be small chemical perturbations and that the manifestations of such perturbations can arise much faster than even the most astute scientists could expect.

Nevertheless, some steps can be taken to counteract rapid atmospheric change, perhaps lessening the known and unknown threats. For example, evidence indicates that a major decrease in the rate of fossil-fuel combustion would slow the greenhouse warming, reduce smog, improve visibility and minimize acid deposition. Other steps could be targeted against particular gases, such as methane. Its emission could be reduced by instituting landfill operations that prevent its release and possibly by adopting less wasteful methods of fossil-fuel production. Methane emission from cattle might even be diminished by novel feeding procedures.

Perhaps more encouraging is the fact that many people and institutions are now aware that their actions can have not only local but also global consequences for the atmosphere and the habitability of the planet. A few recent events exemplify this awareness: in the Montreal protocol of 1987, dozens of nations agreed to halve their chlorofluorocarbon emissions by the end of the century, and several countries and the major chlorofluorocarbon manufacturers have more recently announced their intention to eliminate the chemicals by that deadline. Some of the same nations that have been involved in the Montreal protocol are now discussing the possibility of an international "law of the atmosphere." It would be directed at limiting the release of several greenhouse and chemically active trace gases, including carbon dioxide, methane and nitrous oxide, as well as sulfur dioxide and the NO_x gases.

We and many others think the solution to the earth's environmental problems lies in a truly global effort, involving unprecedented collaboration by scientists, citizens and world leaders. The most technologically developed nations have to reduce their disproportionate use of the earth's resources. Moreover, the developing countries must be helped to adopt environmentally sound technologies and planning strategies as they elevate the standard of living for their populations, whose rapid growth and need for increased energy are a major cause for environmental concern. With proper attention devoted to maintaining the atmosphere's stability, perhaps the chemical changes that are now occurring can be kept within limits that will sustain the physical processes and the ecological balance of the planet.

The Changing Climate

Global warming should be unmistakable within a decade or two. Prompt emission cuts could slow the buildup of heat-trapping gases and limit this risky planetwide experiment.

· · ·

Stephen H. Schneider

In 1957 Roger Revelle and Hans E. Suess of the Scripps Institution of Oceanography observed that humanity is performing a "great geophysical experiment," not in a laboratory, not in a computer, but on our own planet. The outcome of the experiment should be clear within decades, but it essentially began at the start of the Industrial Revolution. Since then human beings have increased the atmospheric content of carbon dioxide by about 25 percent by burning coal, oil and other fossil fuels and by clearing forests, which releases carbon dioxide as the litter is burned or decays.

Carbon dioxide makes up only a thirtieth of 1 percent of the atmosphere, but together with water vapor and other gases present in much smaller quantities, such as methane and the chlorofluorocarbons (CFC's), it plays a major role in determining the earth's climate. As early as the 19th century it was recognized that carbon dioxide in the atmosphere gives rise to a greenhouse effect. The glass of a greenhouse allows sunlight to stream in freely but blocks heat from escaping, mainly by preventing the warm air inside the greenhouse from mixing with outside air. Similarly, carbon dioxide and other greenhouse gases are relatively transparent to sunshine but trap heat by more efficiently absorbing the longer-wavelength infrared radiation released by the earth.

By now the atmosphere's heat-trapping ability has been well established (see Figure 3.2). For example, as seen from space, the earth radiates energy at wavelengths and intensities characteristic of a body at −18 degrees Celsius. Yet the average temperature at the surface is some 33 degrees higher: heat is trapped between the surface and the level, high in the atmosphere, from which radiation escapes. There is virtually no doubt among atmospheric scientists that increasing the concentration of carbon dioxide and other gases will increase the heat trapping and warm the climate.

What, then, is the question that the ongoing geophysical experiment will settle? Even though there is virtually no debate among scientists about the greenhouse effect as a scientific proposition, there is controversy. Will the rising concentrations of green-

Figure 3.1 PARCHED FIELDS turn to sand during a 1983 dry spell in Texas. Such images could multiply if, as several computer models predict, global warming reduces soil moisture in midcontinental regions, where grain production is concentrated.

house gases raise the earth's temperature by one, five or eight degrees C? Will the increase take 50, 100 or 150 years? Will it be drier in Iowa or wetter in India? There is still more controversy when it comes to policy: Should steps be taken to reduce the greenhouse warming or to anticipate its effects? What steps, and when? In the face of so much controversy, an understanding of what is well known, known slightly and not known at all about the greenhouse warming is essential.

Circumstantial evidence from the geologic and historical past bears out a link between climatic change and fluctuations in greenhouse gases. Between 3.5 and four billion years ago the sun is thought to have been about 30 percent fainter than it is today. Yet life evolved and sedimentary rock formed under the faint young sun: at least some of the earth's surface was above the freezing point of water. Some workers have proposed that the early atmosphere contained as much as 1,000 times today's level of carbon dioxide, which compensated for the sun's feeble radiation by its heat-trapping effect.

Later an enhanced greenhouse effect may have been partly responsible for the warmth of the Mesozoic era—the age of the dinosaurs—which fossil evidence suggests was perhaps 10 or 15 degrees C warmer than today. At the time, 100 million years ago and more, the continents occupied different positions than they do now, altering the circulation of the oceans and perhaps increasing the transport of heat from the Tropics to high latitudes. Yet calculations by Eric J. Barron, now at Pennsylvania State University, and others suggest that paleocontinental geography can explain no more than half of the Mesozoic warming.

Increased carbon dioxide can readily explain the extra heating, as Aleksandr B. Ronov and Mikhail I. Budyko of the Leningrad State Hydrological Institute first proposed and as Barron, Starley L. Thompson of the National Center for Atmospheric Research (NCAR) and I have calculated. A geochemical model constructed by Robert A. Berner and Antonio C. Lasaga of Yale University and the late Robert M. Garrels of the University of South Florida suggests that the carbon dioxide may have been released by unusually heavy volcanic activity on the midocean ridges, where new ocean floor is created by upwelling magma [see "The Geochemical Carbon Cycle," by Robert A. Berner and Antonio C. Lasaga; SCIENTIFIC AMERICAN, March, 1989].

Direct evidence linking greenhouse gases with the dramatic climatic changes of the ice ages comes from bubbles of air trapped in the Antarctic ice sheet by the ancient snowfalls that built up to form the ice. A team headed by Claude Lorius of the Laboratory of Glaciology and Geophysics of the Environment, near Grenoble, examined more than 2,000 meters of ice cores—a 160,000-year record—recovered by a Russian drilling project at the Vostok Station in Antarctica (see Figure 3.3). Laboratory analysis of the gases trapped in the core showed that carbon dioxide and methane levels in the ancient atmosphere varied in step with each other and, more important, with the average local temperature (determined from the ratio between hydrogen isotopes in the water molecules of the ice).

During the current interglacial period (the past 10,000 years) and the previous one, a 10,000-year period around 130,000 years ago, the ice recorded a local temperature about 10 degrees C warmer than at the height of the ice ages. (The earth as a whole is about five degrees warmer during interglacials.) At the same time, the atmosphere contained about 25 percent more carbon dioxide and 100 percent more methane than during the glacial periods. It is not clear whether the greenhouse-gas variations caused the climatic changes or vice versa. My guess is that the ice ages were paced by other factors, such as changes in the earth's orbital parameters and the dynamics of ice buildup and retreat, but biological changes and shifts in ocean circulation in turn affected the atmosphere's trace-gas content, amplifying the climatic swings.

A still more detailed record of greenhouse gases and climate comes from the past 100 years, which have seen a further 25 percent increase in carbon dioxide above the interglacial level and another doubling of atmospheric methane. Two groups, one led by James E. Hansen at the National Aeronautics and Space Administration's Goddard Institute for Space Studies and the other by T. M. L. Wigley at the Climatic Research Unit of the University of East Anglia, have constructed records of global average surface temperature for the past century (see Figure 3.4, bottom). The workers drew on data from many of the same recording stations around the globe (the Climatic Research Unit also included readings made at sea), but they had different techniques for analyzing the records and compensating for their shortcomings. Certain recording stations were moved over the course of the century, for example, and readings from city centers may have been skewed

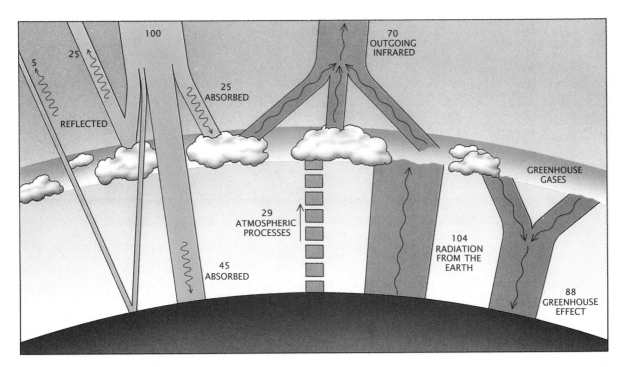

Figure 3.2 HEAT TRAPPING in the atmosphere dominates the earth's energy balance. Some 30 percent of incoming solar energy is reflected (*left*) either from clouds and particles in the atmosphere or from the earth's surface; the remaining 70 percent is absorbed. The absorbed energy is reemitted at infrared wavelengths by the atmosphere (which is also heated by updrafts and cloud formation) and by the surface. Because most of the surface radiation is trapped by clouds and greenhouse gases and returned to the earth, the surface is currently about 33 degrees Celsius warmer than it would be without the trapping.

by heat released by machinery or stored by buildings and pavement.

This "urban heat island" effect is likely to have been disproportionately large in developed countries such as the U.S., but even when the same correction calculated for the U.S. data (by Thomas R. Karl of the National Climatic Data Center in Asheville, N.C., and P. D. Jones of East Anglia) is applied to the global data set, about half a degree C of unexplained "real" warming over the past 100 years remains in both records. In keeping with the trend, the 1980's appear to be the warmest decade on record and 1988, 1987 and 1981 the warmest years, in that order.

Is this the signal of the greenhouse warming? It is tempting to accept it as such, but the evidence is not definitive. For one thing, instead of the steady warming one might expect from a steady buildup of greenhouse gases, the record shows rapid warming until the end of World War II, a slight cooling through the mid-1970's and a second period of rapid warming since then.

What trajectory will the temperature curve follow now? Three basic questions must be answered in forecasts of the climatic future: How much carbon dioxide and other greenhouse gases will be emitted? By how much will atmospheric levels of the gases increase in response to the emissions? What climatic effects will the resulting buildups have, after natural and human factors that might mitigate or amplify those effects are taken into account?

Projecting emissions is an intricate exercise in social science. How much carbon dioxide humanity as a whole will be emitting in the future depends primarily on the global consumption of fossil fuels and the rate of deforestation (which accounts for perhaps half of the buildup since the year 1800 and 20 percent of current emissions). Each factor in turn is

Figure 3.3 ICE CORE—a segment of a two-kilometer core drilled from the Antarctic ice sheet at the Soviet Union's Vostok Station—contains trapped bubbles of ancient air. Analysis of the bubbles and of the ratio of hydrogen isotopes in the ice, which varies with local temperature, enabled Claude Lorius and his colleagues at the Laboratory of Glaciology and Geophysics of the Environment, near Grenoble, to reconstruct a 160,000-year record of trace gases and temperature. (See Figure 3.4. *top*).

affected by many others. Growth in fossil-fuel use, for example, will reflect population growth, the rate at which alternative energy sources and conservation measures are adopted and the state of the world economy. Typical projections assume that global fossil-fuel consumption will continue increasing at about its current pace—much slower than it grew before the energy crisis of the 1970's—yielding increases in carbon dioxide emissions of between .5 and 2 percent a year for the next several decades at least.

Other greenhouse gases, such as methane, the CFC's, oxides of nitrogen and low-level ozone, together could contribute as much to global warming as carbon dioxide, even though they are emitted in much smaller quantities: they are much better at absorbing infrared radiation. But predicting future emissions for these gases is even more complicated than it is for carbon dioxide. The sources of some gases, such as methane, are not well understood; the production of other gases, such as the CFC's and low-level ozone, could rise or fall sharply depending on whether specific technological or policy steps are taken.

Given a plausible scenario for future carbon dioxide emissions, how fast will the atmospheric concentration increase in response? Atmospheric carbon dioxide is continuously being absorbed by green plants and by chemical and biological processes in the oceans (see Figure 3.5). The rate of carbon dioxide uptake is likely to change as the atmospheric concentration changes; that is, feedback processes will enter the equation. Because carbon dioxide is a raw material of photosynthesis, an increased concentration might speed the uptake by plants, counteracting some of the buildup. Similarly, because the carbon dioxide content of the oceans' surface waters stays roughly in equilibrium with that of the atmosphere, oceanic uptake will slow the buildup to some extent. (The slower the buildup is in the first place, the more effective, proportionally, oceanic uptake is likely to be.)

It is also possible, however, that an increased concentration of carbon dioxide and other greenhouse gases will trigger positive feedbacks that would add to the atmospheric burden. Rapid change in climate could disrupt forests and other ecosystems, reducing their ability to draw carbon dioxide down from the atmosphere. Moreover, climatic warming could lead to rapid release of the vast amount of carbon held in the soil as dead organic matter. This stock of carbon—at least twice as much as is stored in the atmosphere—is continuously being decomposed into carbon dioxide and methane by the action of soil microbes. A warmer climate might speed their work, releasing additional carbon dioxide (from dry soils) and methane (from rice paddies, landfills and wetlands) that would en-

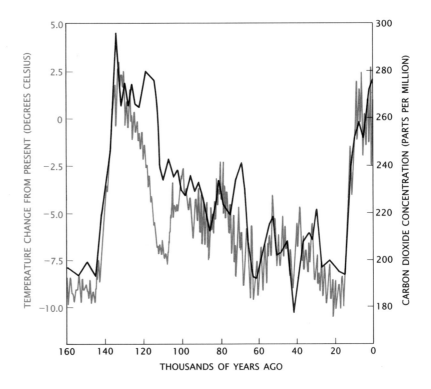

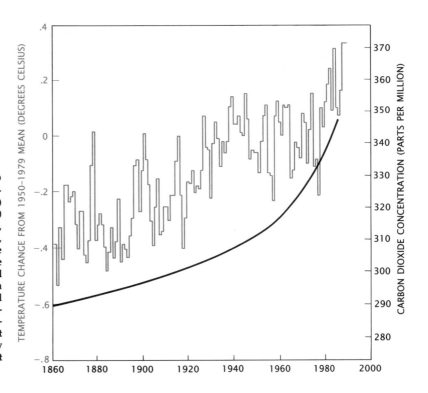

Figure 3.4 CARBON DIOXIDE AND TEMPERATURE are very closely correlated over the past 160,000 years (*top*) and, to a lesser extent, over the past 100 years (*bottom*). The long-term record, based on evidence from Antarctica, shows how the local temperature (*color*) and atmospheric carbon dioxide rose nearly in step as an ice age ended about 130,000 years ago, fell almost in synchrony at the onset of a new glacial period and rose again as the ice retreated about 10,000 years ago. The recent temperature record shows a slight global warming (*color*), as traced by workers at the Climatic Research Unit of the University of East Anglia.

hance the warming. Large quantities of methane are also locked up in continental-shelf sediments and below arctic permafrost in the form of clathrates — molecular lattices of methane and water. Warming of the shallow waters of the oceans and melting of the permafrost could release some of the methane.

In spite of all these uncertainties, many workers expect uptake by plants and by the oceans to moderate the carbon dioxide buildup, at least for the next 50 or 100 years. Typical estimates, based on current or slightly increased emission rates, put the fraction of newly injected carbon dioxide that will remain in the atmosphere at about one half. Under that assumption, the atmospheric concentration will reach 600 parts per million, or about twice the level of 1900, by sometime between the years 2030 and 2080. Some other greenhouse gases are expected to build up faster than carbon dioxide, however.

W hat effect will a doubling of atmospheric carbon dioxide have on climate? The historical record offers no clear quantitative guidance. Nor can climate — the product of complicated interactions involving the atmosphere, the oceans, the land surface, vegetation and polar ice — be physically reproduced in a laboratory experiment. In exploring the future of the earth's climate, my colleagues and I rely on mathematical climate models.

The models, which have been built at Princeton University's Geophysical Fluid Dynamics Laboratory, the Goddard Institute for Space Studies, at NCAR and elsewhere, consist of expressions for the interacting components of the ocean-atmosphere system and equations representing the basic physical laws governing their behavior, such as the ideal gas laws and the conservation of mass, momentum and energy. Given values for, say, the input of energy from the sun and the composition of the atmosphere, a model calculates "climate" — temperature and, in sophisticated models, pressure, wind speed, humidity, soil moisture and other variables.

To keep the task computationally manageable,

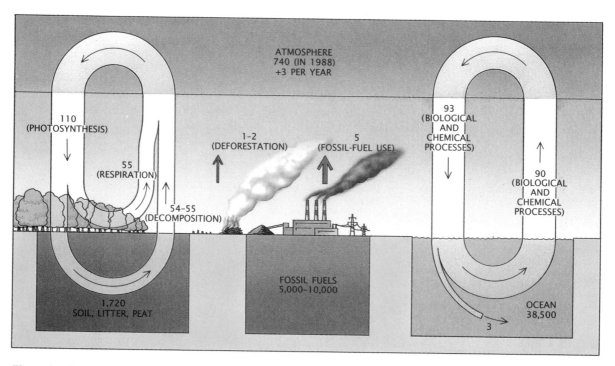

Figure 3.5 CARBON IS EXCHANGED between the atmosphere and reservoirs on the earth. The numbers give the approximate annual fluxes of carbon (in the form of carbon dioxide) and the approximate amount stored in each reservoir in billions of metric tons. The existing cycles — one on land and the other in the oceans — remove about as much carbon from the atmosphere as they add, but human activity (deforestation and fossil-fuel burning) is currently increasing atmospheric carbon by some three billion metric tons yearly. The numbers are based on work by Bert Bolin of the University of Stockholm.

the calculations are done at discrete points in a simplified version of the real world. In the most complicated models—global-circulation models (GCM's), which were first developed for long-term weather forecasts—the atmosphere is represented as a three-dimensional grid with an average horizontal spacing of several hundred kilometers and an average vertical spacing of several kilometers; climate is calculated only at the intersections of the grid lines. In spite of the simplification, running such a GCM for only one simulated year can take many hours on the fastest available supercomputers.

To study the effect of a trace-gas buildup, a modeler simply specifies the projected amount of greenhouse gases and compares the model results with a control simulation of the existing climate, based on the present atmospheric composition. The results of the most recent GCM's are in rough agreement: a doubling of carbon dioxide, or an equivalent increase in other trace gases, would warm the earth's average surface temperature by between 3.0 and 5.5 degrees C. Such a change would be unprecedented in human history; it would match the five-degree warming since the peak of the last ice age 18,000 years ago but would take effect between 10 and 100 times faster.

The shortcomings of computer models limit the reliability of such forecasts. Many processes that affect global climate are simply too small to be seen at the coarse resolution of a model. Such climatically important processes as atmospheric turbulence, precipitation and cloud formation take place on a scale not of hundreds of kilometers (the scale of the grid in a GCM) but of a few kilometers or less. Since such processes cannot be simulated directly, modelers must find a way of relating them to variables that can be simulated on the model's coarse scale. They do so by developing a parameter—a proportionality coefficient—that relates, say, the average cloudiness within a grid cell to the average humidity and temperature (something the model can calculate).

This strategy, known as parameterization, has the effect of aggregating small-scale phenomena that could act as feedbacks on climatic change, either amplifying or moderating it. Clouds, for example, reflect sunlight back to outer space (tending to cool the climate) and also absorb infrared radiation from the earth (tending to warm it). Which effect dominates depends on the clouds' brightness, height, distribution and extent. Recent satellite measurements have confirmed two-decade-old calculations showing that clouds currently have a net cooling

effect; the earth as a whole would be much warmer under cloudless skies (see Figure 3.6). But climatic change might cause incremental changes in cloud characteristics, altering the nature and amount of the feedback. Present models, crudely reproducing only average cloudiness, can say little that is reliable about cloud feedback—or about the many other feedbacks that depend on parameterized processes.

Another shortcoming of present models is their crude treatment of the oceans. The oceans exert potent effects on the present climate and will surely influence climates to come. Their enormous thermal mass will act as a "thermal sponge," slowing any initial increase in global temperature while the oceans themselves warm up. The magnitude of the effect will depend on ocean circulation, which in turn may change as the earth warms. In principle, a climate model should couple a simulated atmosphere with oceans whose dynamics are simulated in equal detail. The computational challenge is staggering, however, and in most GCM's applied to greenhouse warming the dynamics of the oceans are simplified, treated at coarse resolution or left out.

In addition to limiting the reliability of global forecasts, the simplified treatment of the oceans also prevents the models from giving a definitive picture of how climate will change over time in specific regions. Ideally one would like to know not only how much the world as a whole will warm but also whether it will, say, get drier in Iowa, wetter in India or more humid in New York City. Yet, as long as the oceans are out of equilibrium with the atmosphere, their thermal effects will be felt differently at different places. An area in which there is little mixing between surface waters and cold, deep waters might warm quickly; high-latitude regions where deep water is mixed up to the surface might warm more slowly. These thermal effects could in turn affect wind patterns, thereby altering other regional variables, including humidity and rainfall. (Regional forecasts are also compromised in many models by simplified representations of vegetation, which ignore climatically important processes such as the release of water vapor by plants and their effect on surface albedo, or reflectiveness.)

Nevertheless, climatologists have grounds for considerable confidence in their models' forecasts of global surface-temperature change. Individual model elements can be verified by comparing them with the results of a more detailed submodel —a smaller, finer-scale simulation—or with real

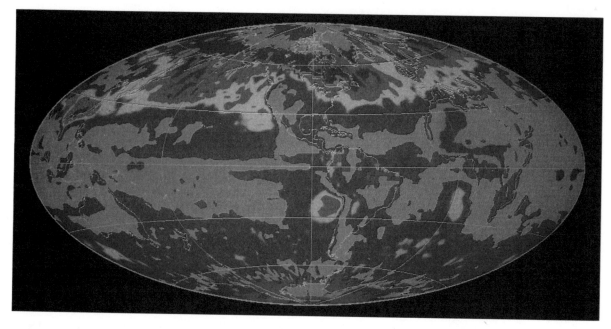

Figure 3.6 CLOUDS AFFECT SURFACE TEMPERA-TURES because they both reflect sunlight, preventing it from warming the earth, and absorb infrared radiation from the surface, contributing to the greenhouse effect. In this image, based on satellite data gathered in April, 1985, clouds had a net cooling effect in some regions (*blues and green*) and a heating effect in others (*red*). On the whole, clouds cool the planet more than they warm it, but the characteristics of clouds and their effect on climate might change unpredictably in a greenhouse world. The image was provided by V. Ramanathan of the University of Chicago.

data. Cloud parameterizations, for example, can be tested against actual measurements of the relation of temperature and humidity to cloudiness within an area corresponding to a cell in the model.

The skill of a model as a whole, and in particular its ability to account for relatively fast processes, such as changes in atmospheric circulation or average cloudiness, can be verified by checking its ability to reproduce the seasonal cycle—a twice-yearly change in hemispheric climate that is larger than any projected greenhouse warming. In spite of parameterization, most GCM's map the seasonal cycle of surface temperature quite well, but their ability to simulate seasonal changes in other climatic variables, including precipitation and relative humidity, has not been studied as thoroughly.

During the course of decades (the expected time scale for unmistakable global warming), other, slower processes that do not affect the seasonal cycle come into play: changes in ocean currents or in the extent of glaciers, for instance. Simulations of past climates—the ice ages or the Mesozoic hot-house—serve as a good check on the long-term accuracy of climate models. To such tests of overall validity can be added simulations of the climates of other planets, such as Venus, where a dense greenhouse atmosphere maintains a surface temperature of about 450 degrees C.

The record of the past 100 years provides the only direct test of the models' ability to simulate the effects of the ongoing greenhouse-gas increase. When a climate model is run for an atmosphere with the composition of 100 years ago and then run again for the historical 25 percent increase in carbon dioxide and doubling in methane, does it "predict" the observed half-degree warming? Actually most models yield a somewhat larger warming, of at least a degree.

If the observed temperature increase really is a greenhouse warming and not just "noise"—a random fluctuation—one might account for the disparity in various ways. Perhaps the models are simply twice too sensitive to small increases in greenhouse gases, or perhaps the incomplete and inhomogeneous network of thermometers has underestimated the global warming. Conceivably some other factor, not well accounted for in the models, is delaying or counteracting the warming. It might be that the heat capacity of the oceans is larger than current models calculate, that the sun's output has declined slightly or that volcanoes have injected more dust into the stratosphere than is currently known, thereby reducing the solar energy reaching the ground.

It may be significant that the transient cooling interrupting the warming trend began around 1940 and was most pronounced in the Northern Hemisphere, coinciding in time and place with a sharp increase in emissions of sulfur from coal- and oil-burning factories and power plants. The sulfur, a major cause of acid rain, is emitted as a gas, sulfur dioxide, but is transformed into fine sulfate particles once in the atmosphere. The particles can travel long distances and serve as condensation nuclei for the formation of cloud droplets, and so they may make some clouds denser and brighter, increasing their cooling effects. In addition, if no soot is bound to the sulfate, it forms a reflective haze even in cloudless skies. Sulfur emissions could be one factor that has held a greenhouse warming down somewhat in the Northern Hemisphere, especially since World War II.

The discrepancy between the predicted warming and what has been seen so far keeps most climatologists from saying with great certainty (99 percent confidence, say) that the greenhouse warming has already taken hold. Yet the discrepancy is small enough, the models are well enough validated and other evidence of greenhouse-gas effects on climate is strong enough, so that most of us believe that the increases in average surface temperature predicted by the models for the next 50 years or so are probably valid within a rough factor of two. (By "probably" I mean it is a better-than-even bet.) Within a decade or so, warming of the predicted magnitude should be clearly evident, even in the noisy global temperature record. But waiting for such conclusive, direct evidence is not a cost-free proposition: by then the world will already be committed to greater climatic change than it would be if action were taken now to slow the buildup of greenhouse gases. Of course, whether or not to act is a value judgment, not a scientific issue.

Why worry about changes in climate on the scale predicted by the models? Changes in temperature and precipitation could threaten natural ecosystems, agricultural production and human settlement patterns. Particular forest types, for example, grow in geographic zones defined largely by temperature. The belt of spruce and fir that now spans Canada grew far to the south at the end of the last ice age 10,000 years ago, hugging the edge of the ice sheet. As the climate warmed by one or two degrees every 1,000 years and the ice retreated, the forest belt migrated northward, at perhaps one kilometer a year. Forests probably could not sustain the much faster migration required by the projected warming, and many ecosystems cannot migrate in any case: they exist only in preserves, which might become marooned in a newly inhospitable climate zone.

Human activities could be affected directly if a warming speeded the evaporation of moisture, reducing stream runoff; in the western U.S. a temperature increase of several degrees C could decrease runoff in the Colorado basin substantially, even if precipitation held steady. As water ran short, faster evaporation would increase the demand for irrigation, adding to the strain on water supplies. At the same time, water quality might suffer as the same waste volume was diluted in lower stream volumes.

What is more, several climate models predict that summer precipitation will actually decline in midcontinental areas, including the central plains of the U.S (see Figure 3.1). The late Dean F. Peterson, Jr., of Utah State University and Andrew A. Keller of Keller-Bliesner Engineering in Logan, Utah, estimated the effects on crop production of a three-degree warming combined with a 10 percent drop in precipitation. They found that based on increased crop water needs and a reduction in available water, the viable acreage in arid regions of the western states and the Great Plains would fall by nearly a third. (A western drying might also result in an increased frequency of wildfires.)

Coastal areas, meanwhile, might face a rise in sea level. Most workers expect a global temperature increase of a few degrees C over the next 50 or 100 years to raise sea level by between .2 and 1.5 meters as a result of the thermal expansion of the oceans, the melting of mountain glaciers and the possible retreat of the Greenland ice sheet's southern margins. (Ice could actually build up in Antarctica owing to warmer winters, which would probably increase snowfall.) The rising sea would endanger coastal settlements and ecosystems and might contaminate groundwater supplies with salt. In spite of many local factors that make it difficult to isolate a consistent global signal, one group of workers recently claimed to have found a uniform worldwide rise in sea level of about two millimeters a year in long-term tide-gauge records. That rise is somewhat larger, however, than one would have expected from the warming seen so far.

Clearly these direct effects of climatic change would have powerful economic, social and political consequences. A decline in agricultural productivity in the Middle West and Great Plains, for example, could be disastrous for farmers and the U.S. economy. By cutting into the U.S. grain surplus, it might also have serious implications for international security.

To be sure, not everyone would lose. If the corn belt simply moved north by several hundred kilometers, for example, Iowa's billion-dollar loss could become Minnesota's billion-dollar gain. But how could the losers be compensated and the winners charged? The issue of equity would become still more thorny if it spanned borders—if the release of greenhouse gases by the economic activities of one country or group of countries did disproportionate harm to other countries whose activities had contributed less to the buildup.

In the face of this array of threats, three kinds of responses could be considered. First, some workers have proposed technical measures to counteract climatic change—deliberately spreading dust in the upper atmosphere to reflect sunlight, for instance. Yet if unplanned climatic changes themselves cannot be predicted with certainty, the effects of such countermeasures would be still more unpredictable. Such "technical fixes" would run a real risk of misfiring—or of being blamed for any unfavorable climatic fluctuations that took place at the same time.

Many economists tend to favor a second class of action: adaptation, often with little or no attempt to anticipate damages or prevent climatic change. Adaptive strategists argue that the large uncertainties in climate projections make it unwise to spend large sums trying to avert outcomes that may never materialize. They argue that adaptation, in contrast, is cheap: the infrastructure that would have to be modified in the face of climatic change—such as water-supply systems and coastal structures—will have to be replaced in any case before large climatic changes are due to appear. The infrastructure can simply be rebuilt as needed to cope with the changing environment.

Passive adaptation relies mostly on reacting to events as they unfold, but some active adaptive steps could be taken now to make future accommodation easier. An American Association for the Advancement of Science panel on climatic change made a strong, potentially controversial but, I believe, compelling suggestion for active adaptation: governments at all levels should reexamine the technical features of water systems and the economic and legal aspects of water-supply management in order to increase the systems' efficiency and flexibility. As the climate warms and precipitation and runoff change, water shortages may grow more common and needs for regional transfers more complex. Even if climate did not change, more flexible water systems would make it easier to cope with the normal extremes of weather.

The third and most active category of response is prevention: curtailing the greenhouse-gas buildup. Energy-conservation measures, alternative energy sources or a switch from coal to natural gas and other fuels with a lower carbon content could all reduce carbon dioxide emissions, as could a halt to deforestation. Stopping the production of CFC's, already notorious because of their ability to erode the stratospheric ozone layer, would eliminate another component of the buildup. A far-reaching proposal for an international framework for reducing emissions was put forward in 1976 by Margaret Mead and William W. Kellogg of NCAR: a "law of the air," which would keep emissions of carbon dioxide below a global standard by assigning polluting rights to each nation.

Proposals for immediate action are controversial because they often entail large immediate investments as insurance against future events whose details are far from certain. Is there some simple principle that can help us to choose which preventive or adaptive measures to spend our resources on? I believe it makes sense to take actions that will yield "tie-in" benefits even if climatic changes do not materialize as forecast.

Pursuing energy efficiency is a good example of this tie-in strategy. More efficient fossil-fuel use will slow the carbon dioxide buildup, but even if the sensitivity of climate to carbon dioxide has been overstated, what would be wasted by taking this step? Efficiency usually makes economic sense, and a reduction in fossil-fuel use would curb acid rain and urban air pollution and lessen the dependence of many countries on foreign producers. Developing alternative energy sources, revising water laws,

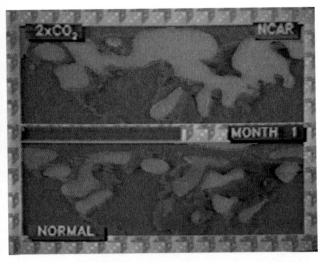

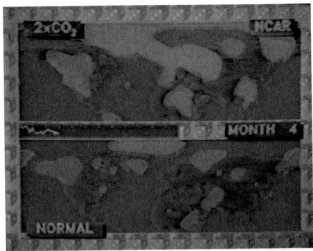

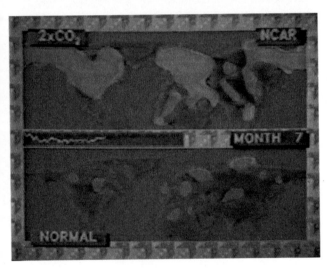

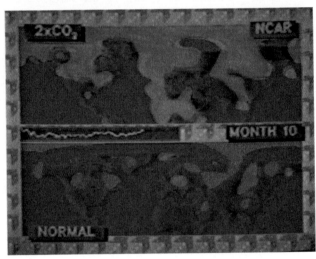

Figure 3.7 SNAPSHOTS OF A GREENHOUSE WORLD come from a climate model used by the author and Starley L. Thompson at the NCAR. The model traced surface temperatures over the year for an atmosphere with twice the present level of carbon dioxide (*top of each frame*); the findings were compared with the results of a yearlong simulation for the present atmosphere (*bottom of each frame*). The red areas were more than six degrees C warmer than the model-calculated normal for that time of year under existing conditions; the light blue areas were more than six degrees colder. The weather anomalies steadily changed position, shape and size, but heating always predominated in the greenhouse simulation.

searching for drought-resistant crop strains, negotiating international agreements on trade in food and other climate-sensitive goods—all these steps could also offer widespread benefits even in the absence of any climatic change.

Often such steps will nonetheless be costly and politically controversial. Regulations or incentives to foster energy-efficient technologies might burden some groups—coal miners and the poor, perhaps —more than others, and the costs may be proportionally greater for poor countries than for rich ones. Actions to prevent a greenhouse warming will have to be coupled with domestic- and foreign-policy measures that attempt to balance fairness and effectiveness. Still, I believe it is better to fight poverty and foster development through direct investment rather than through artificially low energy prices that neglect the costs of the resulting environmental disruptions.

Some people argue that the free market, not government regulation or tax incentives, should dictate increases in energy efficiency, say, or the elimination of CFC's. But it cannot be logically argued that the market is "free" when it does not include some of the potential costs of environmental damage caused by goods or services. Moreover, even political conservatives agree that an economic calculus must give way to a strategic consciousness when national or global security is at stake.

Security is indeed at stake here, as the implications of a global temperature rise of several degrees or more over the next century make clear. Adding to the predicted threats are surprises that may be lurking in the greenhouse century: a sharp positive feedback in the greenhouse-gas buildup from accelerated decay of soil organic matter, dramatic changes in regional climates because of a shift in ocean circulation, or the outbreak of new diseases or agricultural pests as ecosystems are disrupted. In my value system—and this is a political and not a scientific judgment—effective tie-in actions are long overdue.

I am often asked whether I am pessimistic because it will be impossible to avert some global change: at this stage, it appears, no plausible policies are likely to prevent the world from warming by a degree or two. Actually I see a positive aspect: the possibility that a slight but manifest global warming, coupled with the larger threat forecast in computer models, may catalyze international cooperation to achieve environmentally sustainable development, marked by a stabilized population and the proliferation of energy-efficient and environmentally safe technologies. A much larger greenhouse warming (together with many other environmental disruptions) might thereby be averted.

The developed world might have to invest hundreds of billions of dollars every year for many decades, both at home and in financial and technical assistance to developing nations, to achieve a stabilized and sustainable world. It is easy to be pessimistic about the prospects for an international initiative of this scale, but not long ago a massive disengagement of NATO and Warsaw Pact forces in Europe also seemed inconceivable. Disengagement now seems to me to be possible, even likely. Perhaps the resources such an agreement would free and the model of international cooperation it would provide could open the way to a world in which the greenhouse century exists only in the microchips of a supercomputer.

EDITOR'S NOTE

The views expressed in this chapter are not necessarily those of the National Science Foundation, NCAR's sponsor.

Threats to the World's Water

Population growth, ignorance and poverty, along with poor agricultural practices, have endangered water resources. Unless appropriate steps are taken soon, severe shortages will occur.

. . .

J. W. Maurits la Rivière

Water is the earth's most distinctive constituent. It set the stage for the evolution of life and is an essential ingredient of all life today; it may well be the most precious resource the earth provides to humankind. One might therefore suppose that human beings would be respectful of water, that they would seek to maintain its natural reservoirs and safeguard its purity. Yet people in countries throughout the world have been remarkably shortsighted and negligent in this respect. Indeed, the future of the human species and many others may be compromised unless there is significant improvement in the management of the earth's water resources.

All the fresh water in the world's lakes and creeks, streams and rivers represents less than .01 percent of the earth's total store of water. Fortunately, this freshwater supply is continually replenished by the precipitation of water vapor from the atmosphere as rain or snow. Unfortunately, much of that precipitation is contaminated on the way down by gases and particles that human activity introduces into the atmosphere.

Fresh water runs off the land and on its way to the ocean becomes laden with particulate and dissolved matter—both natural detritus and the wastes of human society. When the population density in the catchment area is low, waste matter in the water can be degraded by microbes through a process known as natural self-purification. When the self-purifying capacity of the catchment area is exceeded, however, large quantities of these waste substances accumulate in the oceans, where they can harm aquatic life. The water itself evaporates and enters the atmosphere as pure water vapor. Much of it falls back into the ocean; what falls on land is the precious renewable resource on which terrestrial life depends.

The World Resources Institute estimates that 41,000 cubic kilometers of water per year return to the sea from the land, counterbalancing the atmospheric vapor transport from sea to land (see Figure 4.2). Some 27,000 cubic kilometers, however, return to the sea as flood runoff, which cannot be tapped, and another 5,000 cubic kilometers flow into the sea in uninhabited areas. Of the 41,000 cubic kilometers that return to the sea, some amount is retained on land, where it is absorbed by the vegetation, but the precise amount is not known.

This cycle leaves about 9,000 cubic kilometers readily available for human exploitation worldwide.

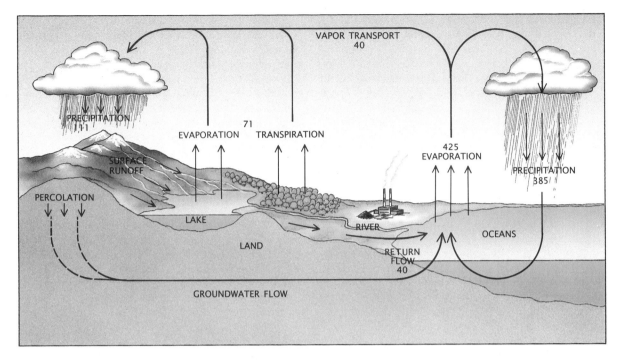

Figure 4.2 GLOBAL WATER CYCLE has three major pathways: precipitation, evaporation and vapor transport. Water precipitates from the sky as rain or snow, most of which (385,000 cubic kilometers per year) falls into the oceans; it returns to the atmosphere by evaporation. Some flows from the land to the sea as runoff or groundwater; in the other direction water vapor is carried by atmospheric currents from the sea to the land. Net flow is measured in thousands of cubic kilometers per year.

That is a plentiful supply of water, in principle enough to sustain 20 billion people. Yet because both the world's population and usable water are unevenly distributed, the local availability of water varies widely (see Figure 4.3). When evaporation and precipitation balances are worked out for each country, water-poor and water-rich countries can be identified. Iceland, for example, has enough excess precipitation to provide 68,500 cubic meters of water per person per year. The inhabitants of Bahrain, on the other hand, have virtually no access

Figure 4.1 OIL HAS LEAKED from a well in Oklahoma to a nearby creek, where it forms a sticky layer on the water's surface and coats the banks. The oil's toxicity has rendered the water uninhabitable to most forms of life, and it is no longer fit for animals to drink. Although this type of oil spill is minor compared with an oil-tanker spill at sea, it is indicative of the wide-ranging impact human activities can have on the world's water supply.

to natural fresh water; they are dependent on the desalinization of seawater. In addition, withdrawal rates per person differ widely from country to country: the average U.S. resident consumes more than 70 times as much water every year as the average resident of Ghana does (see Figure 4.4).

Although the uses to which water is put vary from country to country, agriculture is the main drain on the water supply. Averaged globally, 73 percent of water withdrawn from the earth goes for that purpose. Almost three million square kilometers of land have been irrigated—an area nearly the size of India—and more is being added at the rate of 8 percent a year.

Local water shortages can be solved in two ways. The supply can be increased, either by damming rivers or by consuming capital—by "mining" groundwater. Or known supplies can be conserved, as by increasing the efficiency of irrigation or by relying more on food imports.

In spite of such efforts, there is no doubt that

water is becoming increasingly scarce as population, industry and agriculture all expand. Severe shortages occur as demand exceeds supply. Depletion of groundwater is common in, for example, India, China and the U.S. In the Soviet Union the water level of both the Aral sea and Lake Baikal is dropping dramatically as a result of agricultural and industrial growth in those areas. Contentious competition for the water of such international rivers as the Nile, the Jordan, the Ganges and the Brahmaputra is a symptom of the increasing scarcity of water.

Another problem brought on by overirrigation is salinization. As water evaporates or is taken up by plants, salt is left behind in the soil. The rate of deposition exceeds the rate at which the salt can be removed by flowing water, and so a residue accumulates. Currently more than a million hectares every year are subject to salinization; in the U.S. alone more than 20 percent of the irrigated land is thus affected.

Human activity in a river basin can often aggravate flood hazards. Deforestation and excessive logging lead not only to increased soil erosion but also to increased runoff; in addition, navigation canals are sometimes dug, which may exacerbate flooding by increasing the amount of water that reaches the floodplain.

Finally, of course, any human activity that accentuates the greenhouse effect and ensuing climatic change must inevitably influence the global water cycle. A projected sea-level rise of between .5 and 1.5 meters in the next century, for instance, not only would pose a coastal flooding problem but also would lead to salinization of water resources, create new wetlands while destroying existing ones and increase the ratio of salt water to fresh water on the globe. Precipitation could rise by between 7 and 15 percent in the aggregate; the geographic variations are not predictable.

Assuring an adequate supply is not the only water problem facing many countries throughout the world: they need to worry about water quality. In its passage through the hydrological cycle, water is polluted by two kinds of waste. There is traditional organic waste: human and animal excreta and agricultural fibrous waste (the discarded parts—often more than half—of harvested plants). And there is waste generated by a wide range of industrial processes and by the disposal, after a brief or long lifetime, of industry's products.

Although organic waste is fully biodegradable, it nonetheless presents a significant problem—and in some places a massive one. Excessive biodegradation can cause oxygen depletion in lakes and rivers.

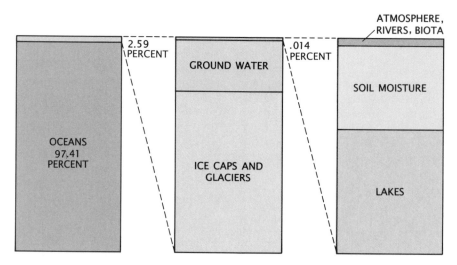

Figure 4.3 DISTRIBUTION OF WATER on the planet is highly uneven. Most of it (97.41 percent) is in the oceans (*gray*); only a small fraction (2.59 percent) is on the land (*blue*). Even most of the water on land is largely unavailable, because it is sequestered in the form of ice and snow or as groundwater; only a tiny amount (.014 percent) of the earth's total water is readily available to human beings and other organisms (*green*).

Human excreta contain some of the most vicious contaminants known, including such pathogenic microorganisms as the waterborne agents of cholera, typhoid fever and dysentery.

Industrial waste can include heavy metals and considerable quantities of synthetic chemicals, such as pesticides. These materials are characterized by toxicity and persistence: they are not readily degraded under natural conditions or in conventional sewage-treatment plants. On the other hand, such industrial materials as concrete, paper, glass, iron and certain plastics are relatively innocuous, because they are inert, biodegradable or at least nontoxic.

Wastes can enter lakes and streams in discharges from such point sources as sewers or drainage pipes or from diffuse sources, as in the case of pesticides and fertilizers in runoff water. Wastes can also be carried to lakes and streams along indirect pathways—for example, when water leaches through contaminated soils and transports the contaminants to a lake or river. Indeed, dumps of toxic chemical waste on land have become a serious source of groundwater and surface-water pollution (see Figure 4.5). The metal drums containing the chemicals are nothing less than time bombs that will go off when they rust through. The incidents at Lekker-

kerk in the Netherlands and at Love Canal in the U.S. are indicators of the pollution of this kind going on worldwide in thousands of chemical-waste dumps.

Some pollutants enter the water cycle by way of the atmosphere. Probably best known among them is the acid that arises from the emission of nitrogen oxides and sulfur dioxide by industry and motor vehicles. Acid deposition, which can be "dry" (as when the gases make direct contact with soil or vegetation) or "wet" (when the acid is dissolved in rain), is causing acidification of low-alkalinity lakes throughout the industrialized world. The acid precipitation also leaches certain positively charged ions out of the soil, and in some rivers and lakes ions can reach concentrations that kill fish.

In areas of intensive animal farming, ammonia released from manure is partly introduced into the atmosphere and partly converted by soil microbes into soluble nitrates in the soil. Since nitrate has high mobility (it is soluble in water and does not bind to soil particles), it has become one of the main pollutants of groundwater, often reaching concentrations that exceed guidelines established by the World Health Organization.

The wind can also carry pollutants—fly ash from coal-burning plants, for example, or sprayed pesti-

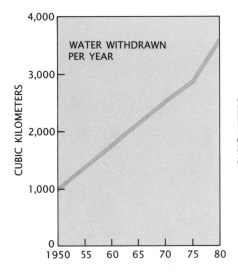

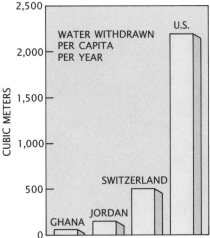

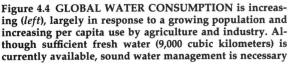

Figure 4.4 GLOBAL WATER CONSUMPTION is increasing (left), largely in response to a growing population and increasing per capita use by agriculture and industry. Although sufficient fresh water (9,000 cubic kilometers) is currently available, sound water management is necessary to ensure an adequate supply for the future. Per capita consumption rates vary drastically (right); the average American, for example, consumes more than 70 times as much water as the average resident of Ghana.

cides. These can be carried great distances, eventually to be deposited on the surfaces of lakes or of rivers.

Another recently recognized aspect of water pollution is the accumulation of heavy metals, nutrients and toxic chemicals in the bottom mud in deltas and estuaries of highly polluted rivers, such as the Rhine. Because of their high pollution content, sediments that are dredged up cannot be used for such projects as landfills in populated or agricultural areas. Moreover, there is always the danger that natural processes or human activity will trigger chemical reactions that mobilize the pollutants by rendering them soluble, thus allowing them to spread over great distances.

T he quality of inland waters depends not only on the amount of waste generated but also on the decontamination measures that have been put into effect. The degree of success in the battle for water quality differs from country to country, but it can be generalized into a conceptual formula proposed by Werner Stumm and his co-workers of the Swiss Federal Institute for Water Resources and Water Pollution Control in Zurich. The formula holds that the contamination load of a river basin depends on the population in the basin, the per capita gross national product (GNP), the effectiveness of decontamination and the amount of river discharge.

Most rivers in the industrialized world, where the population and per capita GNP are stable and decontamination procedures tend to be fairly effective, are nonetheless polluted by both traditional and industrial wastes. Yet some stabilization—if not improvement—of pollution levels was reported in the early 1980's. (Methods for treatment of traditional wastes consist mostly of sedimentation and aerobic and anaerobic microbial degradation, which are intensified forms of natural self-purification.) Methods for degrading inorganic pollutants such as metals and toxic chemicals, although improving, have not been as promising.

Where increasing industrial activity in a river basin has been matched by increasing waste treatment, a decent level of water quality can be maintained (see Figure 4.6). Yet the balance between contamination and decontamination is a precarious one. A serious accidental discharge, such as the one that followed a 1986 fire at a Sandoz factory on the Rhine in Switzerland, is enough to wipe out large numbers of aquatic organisms and force drinking-water purification plants to close their intakes downstream from the accident.

In most newly industrializing countries both organic and industrial river pollution are on the increase, since the annual per capita GNP is rising quickly (as is the population, to a lesser extent) and decontamination efforts are often neglected. In

Figure 4.5 TOXIC-CHEMICAL DUMPS are a serious source of groundwater and surface-water pollution. Illegal dump sites, such as this one in the U.S., are particularly difficult to monitor. Damage occurs when the drums rust through and release their contents, which enter surface waters and eventually percolate down to the groundwater.

these countries industrialization has had higher priority than reduction of pollution. As a consequence, in some regions (East Asia, for example), degradation of water resources is now considered the gravest environmental problem.

In less developed countries, where the population is growing and where waste treatment is practically nonexistent, water pollution by organic wastes is widespread. As a result, millions of people—and children in particular—die each year from water-related diseases that can be prevented by proper sanitation facilities. These countries still suffer from diseases eradicated in the West long ago. Although the United Nations declared the 1980's to be the

International Drinking Water Supply and Sanitation Decade and instituted a program to provide safe drinking water and appropriate sanitation for all by 1990, much remains to be done before the program's ambitious goals are met. Some progress has nonetheless been made in several countries, including Mexico, Indonesia and Ghana.

The quality of the water in lakes is comparable to that in rivers. Thousands of lakes, including some large ones, are currently being subjected to acidification or to eutrophication: the process in which large inputs of nutrients, particularly phosphates, lead to the excessive growth of algae. When the overabundant algae die, their microbial degradation

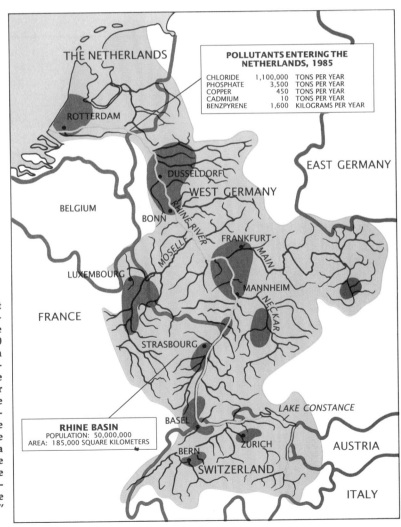

Figure 4.6 RHINE RIVER drains a vast basin (*green*) in four countries—Switzerland, West Germany, France and the Netherlands—as it runs 1,320 kilometers from the Alps to the North Sea. The basin is heavily industrialized (major urban concentrations are shown here in brown), and the river accumulates and transports into the Netherlands a heavy load of pollutants; since 1980 the amounts of some pollutants have been reduced. Now the four countries are cooperating in a Rhine Action Plan intended to improve the quality of the river's water. The primary effort will be to institute recycling within industry as a substitute for after-the-fact "end of pipe" treatment.

POLLUTANTS ENTERING THE NETHERLANDS, 1985

CHLORIDE	1,100,000	TONS PER YEAR
PHOSPHATE	3,500	TONS PER YEAR
COPPER	450	TONS PER YEAR
CADMIUM	10	TONS PER YEAR
BENZPYRENE	1,600	KILOGRAMS PER YEAR

RHINE BASIN
POPULATION: 50,000,000
AREA: 185,000 SQUARE KILOMETERS

consumes most of the dissolved oxygen in the water, vastly reducing the water's capacity to support life. Experience in Europe and North America has shown that the restoration of lakes is possible —at a price—but that the process takes several years. Liming is effective against acidification; flushing out the excess nutrients and restricting the further inflow of nutrients helps to reduce eutrophication.

Although pollution of rivers and lakes is potentially reversible, that is not the case for groundwater. Actually, little is known about the quality of the earth's vast groundwater reserves, except in those instances where particular aquifers are being actively exploited. In Europe and the U.S., where groundwater represents a significant source of fresh water, between 5 and 10 percent of all wells examined are found to have nitrate levels higher than the maximum recommended value of 45 milligrams per liter. Many organic pollutants find their way into groundwater as seepage from waste dumps, leakage from sewers and fuel tanks or as runoff from agricultural land or paved surfaces in proliferating urban and suburban areas.

Because groundwater is cut off from the atmosphere's oxygen supply, its capacity for self-purification is very low: the microbes that normally break down organic pollutants need oxygen to do their job. Prevention of contamination is the only rational approach—particularly for the developing world, where increased reliance on vast groundwater reserves is likely.

The oceans are part of the world's "commons," exploited by many countries and the responsibility of none and therefore all the more difficult to safeguard. More than half of the world's people live on seacoasts, in river deltas and along estuaries and river mouths, and some 90 percent of the marine fish harvest is caught within 320 kilometers of the shore. Every year some 13 billion tons of silt are dumped into coastal zones at the mouths of rivers (see Figure 4.7). Although most of those sediments would have found their way into the ocean anyway, a growing part of the accumulating silt can be attributed to erosion and deforestation caused by human intervention. Depending on the particular agricultural and industrial activities in the catchment area, a coastal zone can be both fertilized and polluted by the silt and dissolved materials that reach it.

The coastal zone is the site of important physicochemical reactions between saltwater and freshwater flows; it is the zone of highest biological productivity, supporting marine life ranging from plankton to fish, turtles and whales. Aquaculture in the coastal zone now produces some 10 percent of the

Figure 4.7 OCEAN POLLUTION is a growing problem, especially in coastal zones. Sewage, which contains abundant nutrients and oxygen-consuming organic matter, is one type of pollutant that can threaten aquatic life, as it has here in the San Francisco Bay.

world's fish harvest. The 240,000 square kilometers of coastal mangrove forest are essential habitats for many economically important fish species during part of their life cycle, and they also provide timber and firewood; reed and cypress swamps are other examples of biologically rich coastal wetlands. Finally, of course, coastal zones support a highly profitable tourist industry and include a growing number of protected areas, such as the Great Barrier Reef Marine Park in Australia.

Aside from river discharges, diffuse runoff, atmospheric transport, waste dumping or burning at sea, offshore mining and shipping accidents are the primary ways that some 20 billion tons of dissolved and suspended matter reach the ocean, where they exert their initial effect on the coastal zone.

Polychlorinated biphenyls (PCB's) and other persistent toxic chemicals, including DDT and heavy-metal compounds, have already spread throughout the world's marine ecosystems, in part through gradual accumulation in the food chain. A ban on the use of DDT and PCB's has been enforced for some 10 years in the industrialized countries and has reduced the concentration of such chemicals in the marine life of North American and European coastal waters. The chemicals are, however, still being used and injected into the marine environment in many tropical regions.

Ocean currents are also vehicles for the transport of trash and pollutants. Examples are the nondegradable plastic bottles, pellets and containers that now commonly litter beaches and the ocean's surface. They cause the death of thousands of birds, fish and marine mammals that mistake them for food or get entangled in them. Less spectacular but possibly more serious are the chemical and biological processes (as yet poorly understood) whereby toxic substances such as radioactive wastes are distributed and accumulated.

Excessive sewage discharges from coastal urban areas lead to eutrophication of coastal waters, which can change the composition of plankton populations. The plankton, provided with abundant nutrients in the sewage, may experience rapid population growth, which depletes the supply of available oxygen and so leads to fish kills. Moreover, the presence of pathogenic bacteria in sewage has forced the closing of many kilometers of beaches to swimmers and has led to prohibitions on the harvesting of shellfish, which concentrate the bacteria in their tissues.

About one tenth of 1 percent of the world's total annual oil production—some five million tons a year, or more than one gram per 100 square meters of the ocean's surface—finds its way to the ocean. Large areas of the ocean would be covered with oil accumulated over the past decades were it not for the fact that the oil eventually evaporates or is degraded by bacteria. Although petroleum is almost entirely biodegradable, it takes the microbes that break it down a long time to accomplish the task, because their activity is limited by the low nutrient concentrations in seawater. In the meantime an oil spill's effects are lethal for a variety of plankton, fish larvae and shellfish, as well as for such larger animals as birds and marine mammals (see Figure 4.1).

It is clear that the quality of the water in coastal zones is seriously endangered and that damage to fisheries and marine wildlife is widespread. Regional seas such as the Baltic and the Mediterranean, which have more coastline per square kilometer than the high seas do, suffer more from water pollution. Their poor condition demonstrates what may happen in the future to the larger oceans of the world.

Human activity is clearly responsible for widespread damage to marine ecosystems. What is not firmly established is how quickly toxic substances can accumulate in marine organisms or whether such accumulation is reversible. Nor has it been determined precisely how synthetic chemicals are transported through the oceans and what the likelihood is that toxic substances in bottom sediments will find their way into the human food supply. Yet experience so far dictates utmost caution, the more so because restoration of the oceans is incomparably more difficult than that of lakes and inland seas, if not impossible.

Some management of water resources—of both their quantity and quality—is now widely practiced all over the world, but the results, particularly in quality control, have so far been inadequate (see Figure 4.8). All signals point to further deterioration in the quality of fresh and marine waters unless more aggressive management programs are instituted.

Many of the guiding principles in water management have evolved from past experience and are well known, and yet their application has lagged. Above all, the need for an integrated approach has become apparent. In every river or lake basin, socio-economic and environmental aspirations must be orchestrated so that human settlements, industry, energy production, agriculture, forests, fisheries and wildlife can coexist. In many cases varied interests are not necessarily in conflict; they can be synergistic. Erosion control, for example, goes hand in hand with reforestation, flood prevention and water conservation.

An integrated approach calls, of course, for closer cooperation at the governmental and intergovernmental level; it goes against the historical allocation of different tasks to different agencies. In many countries water supply and sanitation are handled by separate departments. Departmental budgets are isolated by money-tight walls, making it hard to balance investments made by one department with any resulting gains or savings accrued to another.

Such obstacles are even more formidable in an international setting. A country is unlikely to make significant investments in the decontamination of a river's water if it is other countries, downstream, that are likely to reap the benefits. The less developed countries may actually have a better opportunity to make progress here than the developed ones, where vested interests have entrenched themselves in rigid administrative structures. The United Nations Environment Program (UNEP), for example,

has drawn up an action plan for the Zambezi River based largely on principles of integrated management.

A water-management project should lean toward increasing the efficiency of water consumption rather than toward increasing the supply of water. To increase the supply is often more costly, and in any case it merely postpones a crisis. Indeed, because many countries are already overtaxing their water reserves, increasing efficiency is the only solution in some cases. Irrigation, for example, is terribly inefficient as it is practiced in most countries. Averaged over the world, only about 37 percent of all irrigation water is taken up by crops; the rest is never absorbed by the plants and can be considered lost. New microirrigation techniques, by which perforated pipes deliver water directly to the plants, provide great opportunities for water conservation, making it possible to expand irrigated fields without building new dams (see Figure 4.9).

The mining of groundwater in order to increase supply should, of course, be avoided at all costs—

Figure 4.8 WATER DECADE, a water-quality program launched by the United Nations, aims to provide the people of the world with safe drinking water and appropriate sanitation by the 1990's. The photograph, which was taken **in 1983, depicts a woman drawing drinking water from a new well in Mali. Despite the program's best intentions, however, water quality is still a pressing problem in many parts of the world.**

unless it can be guaranteed that the aquifer from which the water is taken will be replenished. The protection of groundwater quality also deserves special attention. Government officials are more likely to implement pollution-control measures when they (or their constituents) are presented with highly visible signs of pollution, such as rubbish washed onto a beach. Hidden as it is from view, groundwater can therefore become polluted gradually without eliciting an outcry from the public until it is too late to reverse the damage wrought by the pollution.

It has also become apparent that the prevention of pollution, and the restoration of bodies of water that are already polluted, should gradually take precedence over the development of purification technologies. Water-purifying technology is becoming more complex and costly as the number of pollutants in water increases; the money spent on removing contaminants from drinking water would be better spent on preventing the contaminants from entering the water in the first place. The high cost of restoring polluted water bodies also strengthens the appeal of pollution prevention programs.

For that reason "end of pipe" remedies for indus-

Figure 4.9 NEW MICROIRRIGATION TECHNIQUES make it possible to send water directly to the roots of individual plants. They represent a major advance in water conservation because they provide only about as much water as the plants actually need. This system is watering a cotton crop in central Texas, an arid region where the efficiency of microirrigation has enabled farmers to rely less on groundwater for irrigation.

trial water pollution should be replaced by recycling and reuse. Factories designed to minimize water pollution through waste reduction are often more economic than those that construct their own waste-water treatment plants in order to meet environmental standards. Factories that integrate pollution-control techniques are also likely to be more acceptable to an environmentally conscious populace. As Peter Donath of the Ciba-Geigy Corporation, one of the world's largest chemical companies, said at last year's International Rhine Conference, "Only with environmentally sound products and manufacturing processes will the chemical industry be able to maintain social acceptability in the future." As an example of this new trend in chemical engineering, he cited a novel process for the production of naphthalene sulfonic acids that reduces pollution by more than 90 percent.

Pollution of a river or a regional sea is, of course, more easily perceived than the pollution of the oceans, which are much larger; it is not surprising that the UNEP has already established pollution-control programs for 10 regional seas. Although such programs are a good start, they need to be followed up with protection of the oceans in general. A recent step in this direction is an international agreement forbidding the discarding of plastics from ships, which became effective at the beginning of this year. Other existing international conventions regulating marine resources need to be improved by backing them up with better monitoring schemes and enforcement measures.

Parallel with the need for improved water-resources management is the need for more research on the hydrosphere. For example, ecological and toxicologic studies of marine life are badly needed if we are to improve the husbandry of the oceans and gain better understanding of the ecological effects of long-lived pollutants in ocean waters.

Many aspects of the hydrological cycle, including the fluxes between its compartments and the extent of groundwater reserves, are not accurately known. These problems and others are currently being addressed by the International Hydrological Program of the United Nations Educational, Scientific and Cultural Organization. Moreover, major international research programs to study the interactions between climate and the hydrological cycle have recently been launched by the UNEP as well as by the World Health Organization and the nongovernmental International Council of Scientific Unions.

Predicting what is likely to happen if sound principles of water management are not vigorously implemented is all too easy. We have already seen rivers turn into sewers and lakes into cesspools. People die from drinking contaminated water, pollution washes ashore on recreational beaches, fish are poisoned by heavy metals and wildlife habitats are destroyed. A laissez-faire approach to water management will spell more of the same—on a grander scale. One can only hope recognition of that fact will spur governments and people into action.

Threats to Biodiversity

Habitat destruction, mostly in the tropics, is driving thousands of species each year to extinction. The consequences will be dire—unless the trend is reversed.

. . .

Edward O. Wilson

The human species came into being at the time of greatest biological diversity in the history of the earth. Today as human populations expand and alter the natural environment, they are reducing biological diversity to its lowest level since the end of the Mesozoic era, 65 million years ago. The ultimate consequences of this biological collision are beyond calculation and certain to be harmful. That, in essence, is the biodiversity crisis.

In one sense the loss of diversity is the most important process of environmental change. I say this because it is the only process that is wholly irreversible. Its consequences are also the least predictable, because the value of the earth's biota (the fauna and flora collectively) remains largely unstudied and unappreciated. Every country can be said to have three forms of wealth: material, cultural and biological. The first two we understand very well, because they are the substance of our everyday lives. Biological wealth is taken much less seriously. This is a serious strategic error, one that will be increasingly regretted as time passes. The biota is on the one hand part of a country's heritage, the product of millions of years of evolution centered on that place and hence as much a reason for national concern as the particularities of language and culture. On the other hand, it is a potential source for immense untapped material wealth in the form of food, medicine and other commercially important substances.

It is a remarkable fact, given the interdependence of human beings and the other species that inhabit the planet, that the task of studying biodiversity is still in an early stage. Although systematics is one of the two oldest formal disciplines of biology (the other is anatomy), we do not even know to the nearest order of magnitude the number of species of organisms on the earth. With the help of other specialists, I have estimated the number of species that have been formally described (given a Latinized scientific name) to be about 1.4 million. Even conservative guesses place the actual number of species at four million or greater, more than twice the number described to date.

Terry L. Erwin of the Smithsonian's National Museum of Natural History believes the number of species to be even greater. With the help of coworkers, he applied an insecticidal fog to the forest canopy at localities in Brazil and Peru in order to obtain an estimate of the total number of insect and other arthropod species in this rich but still relatively unexplored habitat. By extrapolating his findings to moist tropical forests around the world and

by including a rough estimate of the number of ground-dwelling species in his calculations, Erwin arrived at a global total of 30 million species. Even if this number proves to be a considerable overestimate, the amount of biodiversity in the world is certain to be projected sharply upward in other, compensatory ways.

Groups such as the mites and fungi, for example, are extremely rich and also very underexplored, and habitats such as the floors of the deep sea are thought to harbor hundreds of thousands of species, most of which remain undescribed. Even the number of bacterial species on the earth is expected to be many times greater than the 3,000 that have been characterized to date. To take one example, an entirely new flora of bacteria has recently been discovered living at depths of 350 meters or more beneath the ground near Hilton Head, South Carolina. Even new species of birds continue to turn up at an average rate of two per year.

Systematists are in wide agreement that whatever the absolute numbers, more than half of the species on the earth live in moist tropical forests, popularly referred to as rain forests (see Figure 5.1). Occupying only 6 percent of the land surface, these ecosystems are found in warm areas where the rainfall is 200 centimeters or more per year, which allows broad-leaved evergreen trees to flourish. The trees typically sort into three or more horizontal layers, the canopy of the tallest being 30 meters (about 100 feet) or more from the ground. Together the tree crowns of the several layers admit little sunlight to the forest floor, inhibiting the development of undergrowth and leaving large spaces through which it is relatively easy to walk.

The belief that a majority of the planet's species live in tropical rain-forest habitats is not based on an exact and comprehensive census but on the fact that the two overwhelmingly species-rich groups, the arthropods (especially insects) and the flowering plants, are concentrated there. Other extremely species-rich environments exist, including the coral reefs and abyssal plains of the oceans and the heathlands of South Africa and southwestern Australia, but these appear to be outranked substantially by the rain forests.

Every tropical biologist has stories of the prodigious variety in this one habitat type. From a single leguminous tree in Peru, I once retrieved 43 ant species belonging to 26 genera, approximately equal to the ant diversity of all of the British Isles (see Figure 5.2). In 10 selected one-hectare plots in Kalimantan in Indonesia, Peter S. Ashton of Harvard University found more than 700 tree species, about equal to the number of tree species native to all North America. The current world record at this writing (certain to be broken) was established in 1988 by Alwyn H. Gentry of the Missouri Botanical Garden, who identified approximately 300 tree species in each of two one-hectare plots near Iquitos, Peru.

Why has life multiplied so prodigiously in a few limited places such as tropical forests and coral reefs? It was once widely believed that when large numbers of species coexist, their life cycles and food webs lock together in a way that makes the ecosystem more robust. This diversity-stability hypothesis has given way during the past 20 years to a reversed cause-and-effect scenario that might be called the stability-diversity hypothesis: fragile superstructures of species build up when the environment remains stable enough to support their evolution during long periods of time. Biologists now know that biotas, like houses of cards, can be brought tumbling down by relatively small perturbations in the physical environment. They are not robust at all.

The history of global diversity is reflected in the standing diversity of marine animals, the group best represented in the fossil record. The trajectory can be summarized as follows: after the initial "experimental" flowering of multicellular animals, there was a swift rise in species number in early Paleozoic times (some 600 million years ago), then plateaulike stagnation for the remaining 200 million years of the Paleozoic era and finally a slow but steady climb through the Mesozoic and Cenozoic eras to diversity's present all-time high (see Figure 5.3).

The overall impression gained from examining these and comparable sets of data for other groups of organisms is that biological diversity was hard won and a long time in coming. Furthermore, the

Figure 5.1 TROPICAL RAIN FORESTS, such as this one in northern Costa Rica, are among the most species-rich habitats on the earth. The enormous biological diversity found in these forests can be explained by the fact that the most species-rich groups on the planet, the invertebrates and flowering plants, are concentrated there. The vegetation, much of it broad-leaved evergreens, is extremely lush; the tallest trees tower as much as 30 meters (100 feet) above the rain-forest floor.

Figure 5.2 INSECT DIVERSITY is extraordinarily high in tropical rain forests, where millions of species, including this ant from the island of Sulawesi in Indonesia, have yet to be inventoried. The ant, which is unusual for its large eyes and robotlike movements, belongs to the genus *Opisthopsis* but has not yet been given a species name.

procession of life was set back by five massive extinction episodes during the Ordovician, Devonian, Permian, Triassic and Cretaceous periods. The last of these is by far the most famous, because it ended the age of dinosaurs, conferred hegemony on the mammals and ultimately, for better or worse, made possible the origin of our own species. But the Cretaceous crisis was minor compared with the great Permian crash some 240 million years ago, which extinguished between 77 and 96 percent of all marine animal species. As David M. Raup of the University of Chicago has observed, "If these estimates are even reasonably accurate, global biology (for higher organisms, at least) had an extremely close call." It took five million years, well into Mesozoic times, for species diversity to begin a significant recovery.

What lessons can be drawn from these extinction episodes of the past? It is clear that recovery, given sufficient time, is sometimes possible. It is also true that in some cases new species can be created rapidly. A large minority of flowering-plant species have originated in a single generation by polyploidy—a multiplication of chromosome sets, either within a single individual or following the hybridization of two previously distinct species. Even geographic speciation, in which populations diverge genetically after being separated by a barrier such as a strait or desert, can in extreme cases lead to the evolution of new species in as few as

from 10 to 100 generations. Hence, it might be argued that when a mass extinction occurs the deficit can be made up in a relatively short time. But under such circumstances pure *numbers* of species mean little. What matters more, in terms of the spread of genetic codes and the multiple ways of life they prescribe, is diversity at the higher taxonomic levels: the number of genera, families and so on.

A species is most interesting when its traits are sufficiently unique to warrant its placement in a distinct genus or even a higher-level taxon, such as a family. A concrete example helps to illustrate my point. In western China a new species of muntjac deer was recently discovered, which appears to differ from the typical muntjac of Asia only in chromosome number and in a few relatively minor anatomical traits. Human beings intuitively value this slightly differentiated species, of course, but not nearly so much as they value the giant panda, which is so distinctive as to be placed in its own genus (*Ailuropoda*) and family (Ailuropodidae).

Within the past 10,000 years biological diversity has entered a wholly new era in the turbulent history of life on the earth. Human activity has had a devastating effect on species diversity, and the rate of human-induced extinctions is accelerating. The heaviest pressure has hitherto been exerted on islands, lakes and other isolated and strongly circumscribed environments. Fully one half

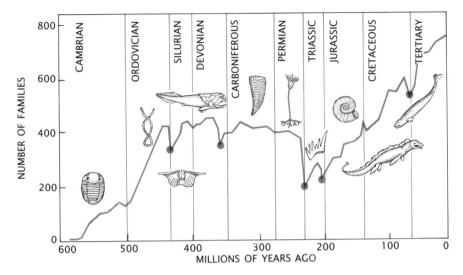

Figure 5.3 BIOLOGICAL DIVERSITY has increased slowly over time, set back occasionally by mass-extinction events: at the close of the Ordovician, Devonian, Permian, Triassic and Cretaceous periods, when the number of families of marine organisms declined by 12, 14, 52, 12 and 11 percent, respectively. The extinction event at the end of the Permian was by far the most severe; since then diversity has slowly increased to its present all-time high. It is now declining at an unprecedented rate, however, as a result of human activity.

of the bird species of Polynesia have been eliminated through hunting and the destruction of native forests. In the 1800's most of the unique flora of trees and shrubs on St. Helena, a tiny island in the South Atlantic, was lost forever when the island was completely deforested. Hundreds of fish species that are endemic to Lake Victoria, formerly of great commercial value as food and aquarium fish, are now threatened with extinction as the result of the careless introduction of one species of fish, the Nile perch. The list of such biogeographic disasters is extensive.

Serious as the episodes of pinpoint destruction are, they are minor compared with the species hecatomb caused by the clearing and burning of tropical rain forests. Already the forest has been reduced to approximately 55 percent of its original cover (as inferred from soil and climate profiles of the land surface), and it is being further reduced at a rate in excess of 100,000 square kilometers a year. This amount is 1 percent of the total cover, or more than the area of Switzerland and the Netherlands combined.

What is the effect of such habitat reduction on species diversity? In archipelago systems such as the West Indies and Polynesia, the number of species found on an individual island corresponds roughly to the island's area: the number of species usually increases with the size of the island, by somewhere between the fifth and the third root of the area (see Figure 5.4). Many fall close to the central value of the fourth root. The same relation holds for "habitat islands," such as patches of forest surrounded by a sea of grassland. As a rough rule of thumb, a tenfold increase in area results in a doubling of the number of species. Put the other way, if the island area is diminished tenfold, the number of species will be cut in half.

The theory of island biogeography, which has been substantiated at least in broad outline by experimental alterations of island biotas and other field studies, holds that species number usually fluctuates around an equilibrium. The number remains more or less constant over time because the rate of immigration of new species to the island balances the extinction rate of species already there, and so diversity remains fairly constant. The relation between the theory of island biogeography and global diversity is an important one: if the area of a particular habitat, such as a patch of rain forest, is reduced by a given amount, the number of species living in it will subside to a new, lower equilibrium. The rich forest along the Atlantic coast of Brazil, for example, has been cleared to less than 1 percent of its original cover; even in the unlikely event that no more trees are cut, the forest biota can be expected to decline by perhaps 75 percent, or to one quarter of its original number of species.

I have conservatively estimated that on a world-wide basis the ultimate loss attributable to rain-forest clearing alone (at the present 1 percent rate) is from .2 to .3 percent of all species in the forests per year. Taking a very conservative figure of two million species confined to the forests, the global loss that results from deforestation could be as much as from 4,000 to 6,000 species a year. That in turn is on the order of 10,000 times greater than the naturally occurring background extinction rate that existed prior to the appearance of human beings.

Although the impact of habitat destruction is most severely felt in tropical rain forests, where species diversity is so high, it is also felt in other regions of the planet, particularly where extensive forest clearing is taking place (see Figure 5.5). In the U.S. alone, some 60,000 acres of ancient forests are being cut per year, mostly for lumber that is then exported to Japan and other countries in the Pacific rim. Most severely affected are the national forests of the Pacific Northwest, from which some 5.5 billion board-feet of timber were harvested in 1987, and Alaska's Tongass National Forest, where as much as 50 percent of the most productive forest-land has been logged since 1950 (see Figure 5.6). Although reforestation in these areas is possible, the

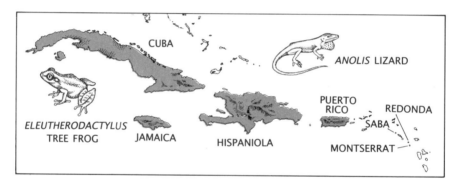

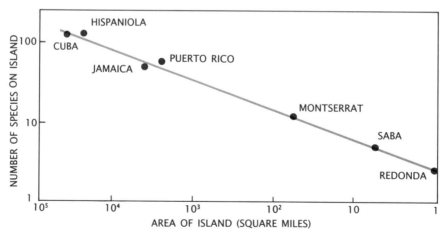

Figure 5.4 NUMBER OF SPECIES on an island corresponds to its size. As a general rule, when the area of an island increases tenfold, the number of species on it doubles. This is easily demonstrated for an island archipelago, such as the West Indies (*top*), where there are numerous islands of different sizes. The numbers of species of reptiles and amphibians on five islands, including *Anolis* lizards and *Eleutherodactylus* tree frogs, were counted and the combined total plotted against the area of each island. As the curve shows (*bottom*), a large island, such as Cuba, has more than twice as many species as, say, the smaller island of Saba. These findings can be used to predict species loss from habitat destruction.

Figure 5.5 DEFORESTATION IS OCCURRING at a rapid rate around the world. In Costa Rica (*top*), rain forest is often cut and the land fenced in and converted to pasture. Tropical forests typically have poor-quality soil, and within two or three years after being cleared, soil that once supported dense vegetation becomes too nutrient-poor to provide much grass for grazing cattle. In the U.S. (*bottom*), the impact of large-scale logging operations can be clearly seen in this mountain range in the state of Washington. The scattered logs in the foreground are trees that have been cut and stripped of their branches and are waiting to be collected.

the process of regrowth may possibly last 100 years or more.

How long does it take, once a habitat is reduced or destroyed, for the species that live in it to actually become extinct? The rate of extinction depends on the size of the habitat patch left undisturbed and the group of organisms concerned. In one ingenious study, Jared M. Diamond of the University of California at Los Angeles and John W. Terborgh of Duke University counted the number of bird species on several continental-shelf islands, which until about 10,000 years ago had been part of the mainland but then became isolated when the sea level rose. By comparing the number of species per island with the number of species on the adjacent mainland, Diamond and Terborgh were able to estimate the number of species each island had lost and to correlate the rate of species loss with island size.

Their model has been reasonably well confirmed by empirical studies of local bird faunas, and the results are sobering: in patches of between one and 20 square kilometers, a common size for reserves and parks in the tropics and elsewhere, 20 percent or more of the species disappear within 50 years. Some of the birds vanish quickly. Others linger for a while as the "living dead." In regions where the natural habitat is highly fragmented, the rate of species loss is even greater.

These extinction rates are probably underestimates, because they are based on the assumption that the species are distributed more or less evenly throughout the forests being cut. But biological surveys indicate that large numbers of species are confined to very limited ranges; if the small fraction of the forest habitat occupied by a species is destroyed, the species is eliminated immediately. When a single ridge top in Peru was cleared recently, more than 90 plant species known only from that locality were lost forever.

Ecologists have begun to identify "hot spots" around the world—habitats that are rich in species and also in imminent danger of destruction.

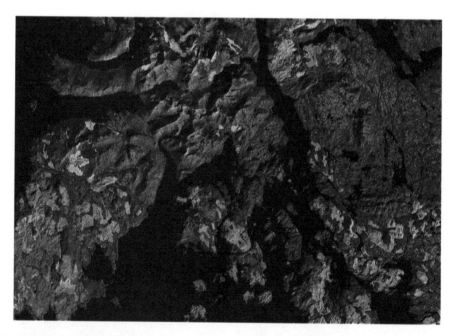

Figure 5.6 SATELLITE IMAGE of the northern tip of Prince of Wales Island in Tongass National Forest, Alaska, shows the extent to which the region has been clear cut. Areas that have recently been cleared and are barren of tree cover are indicated in pink; those that have been cut but have started to recover are light green; areas where the forest has not yet been disturbed are dark green. The image covers about 400 square miles.

Norman Myers, an environmental consultant with wide experience in the tropics, has compiled a list of threatened rain-forest habitats from 10 places: the Chocó of western Colombia, the uplands of western Amazonia, the Atlantic coast of Brazil, Madagascar, the eastern Himalayas, the Philippines, Malaysia, northwestern Borneo, Queensland and New Caledonia. Other biologists have similarly classified certain temperate forest patches, heathlands, coral reefs, drainage systems and ancient lakes. One of the more surprising examples is Lake Baikal in Siberia, where large numbers of endemic crustaceans and other invertebrates are endangered by rising levels of pollution.

The world biota is trapped as though in a vise. On one side it is being swiftly reduced by deforestation. On the other it is threatened by climatic warming brought on by the greenhouse effect. Whereas habitat loss is most destructive to tropical biotas, climatic warming is expected to have a greater impact on the biotas of the cold temperate regions and polar regions. A poleward shift of climate at the rate of 100 kilometers or more per century, which is considered at least a possibility, would leave wildlife preserves and entire species ranges behind, and many kinds of plants and animals could not migrate fast enough to keep up.

The problem would be particularly acute for plants, which are relatively immobile and do not disperse as readily as animals. The Engelmann spruce, for example, has an estimated natural dispersal capacity of from one to 20 kilometers per century, so that massive new plantings would be required to sustain the size of the range it currently occupies. Margaret Davis and Catherine Zabinski of the University of Minnesota predict that in response to global warming four North American trees — yellow birch, sugar maple, beech and hemlock — will be displaced northward by from 500 to 1,000 kilometers. Hundreds of thousands of species are likely to be similarly displaced; how many will adapt to the changing climate, not having migrated, and how many will become extinct is, of course, unknown.

Virtually all ecologists, and I include myself among them, would argue that every species extinction diminishes humanity. Every microorganism, animal and plant contains on the order of from one million to 10 billion bits of information in its genetic code, hammered into existence by an astronomical number of mutations and episodes of natural selection over the course of thousands or millions of years of evolution. Biologists may eventually come to read the entire genetic codes of some individual

Figure 5.7 **PLANTS FROM TROPICAL RAIN FORESTS** are the source of food, medicine and other commercially valuable products. The rosy periwinkle, *Catharanthus roseus* (*left*), contains substances that are effective against some cancers, and the babassú palm, *Orbignya phalerata* (*right*), produces bunches of fruit (each one weighing about 200 pounds), from which oil (for cooking and other purposes) can be extracted.

strains of a few of the vanishing species, but I doubt that they can hope to measure, let alone replace, the natural species and the great array of genetic strains composing them. The power of evolution by natural selection may be too great even to conceive, let alone duplicate. Without diversity there can be no selection (either natural or artificial) for organisms adapted to a particular habitat that then undergoes change. Species diversity—the world's available gene pool—is one of our planet's most important and irreplaceable resources. No artificially selected genetic strain has, to my knowledge, ever outcompeted wild variants of the same species in the natural environment.

It would be naive to think that humanity need only wait while natural speciation refills the diversity void created by mass extinctions. Following the great Cretaceous extinction (the latest such episode), from five to 10 million years passed before diversity was restored to its original levels. As species are exterminated, largely as a result of habitat destruction, the capacity for natural genetic regeneration is greatly reduced. In Norman Myers's phrase, we are causing the death of birth.

Wild species in tropical forests and other natural habitats are among the most important resources available to humankind, and so far they are the least utilized. At present, less than one tenth of 1 percent of naturally occurring species are exploited by human beings, while the rest remain untested and fallow. In the course of history people have utilized about 7,000 plant species for food, but today they rely heavily on about 20 species, such as wheat, rye, millet and rice—plants for the most part that Neolithic man encountered haphazardly at the dawn of agriculture. Yet at least 75,000 plant species have edible parts, and at least some of them are demonstrably superior to crop species in prevalent use. For example, the winged bean, *Psophocarpus tetragonolobus*, which grows in New Guinea, has been called a one-species supermarket: the entire plant—roots, seeds, leaves, stems and flowers—is edible, and a coffeelike beverage can be made from its juice. It grows rapidly, reaching a height of 15 feet in a few weeks, and has a nutritional value equal to that of soybeans.

Wild plant and animal species also represent vast reservoirs of such potentially valuable products as fibers and petroleum substitutes. One example is the babassú palm, *Orbignya phalerata*, from the Am-

azon basin; a stand of 500 trees produces about 125 barrels of oil a year. Another striking example is the rosy periwinkle, *Catharanthus roseus*, an inconspicuous little plant that originated in Madagascar. It yields two alkaloids, vinblastine and vincristine, that are extremely effective against Hodgkin's disease and acute lymphocytic leukemia (see Figure 5.7). The income from these two substances alone exceeds $100 million a year. Five other species of *Catharanthus* occur on Madagascar, none of which have been carefully studied. At this moment one of the five is close to extinction due to habitat destruction.

Biological diversity is eroding at a swift pace, and massive losses can be expected if present rates continue. Can steps be taken to slow the extinction process and eventually bring it to a halt? The answer is a guarded "yes." Both developed and developing (mostly tropical) countries need to expand their taxonomic inventories and reference libraries in order to map the world's species and identify hot spots for priority in conservation. At the same time, conservation must be closely coupled with economic development, especially in countries where poverty and high population densities threaten the last of the retreating wildlands. Biologists and economic planners now understand that merely setting aside reserves, without regard for the needs of the local population, is but a short-term solution to the biodiversity crisis.

Recent studies indicate that even with a limited knowledge of wild species and only a modest effort, more income can often be extracted from sustained harvesting of natural forest products than from clear-cutting for timber and agriculture. The irony of cutting down tropical forests in order to grow crops or graze cattle is that after two or three years the nutrient-poor topsoil can no longer support the agricultural activity for which it was cleared in the first place.

Thomas Eisner of Cornell University has suggested that in addition to the compilation of biological inventories, programs should be established to promote chemical prospecting around the world as part of the search for new products. The U.S. National Cancer Institute has begun to do just that: their natural products branch is currently screening some 10,000 substances a year for activity against cancer cells and the AIDS virus.

It has become equally clear that biological research must be tied to zoning and regional land-use planning designed not only to conserve and promote the use of wild species but also to make more efficient use of land previously converted to agriculture and monoculture timber. More efficient land use includes choosing commercial species well suited to local climatic and soil conditions, planting mixtures of species with yields higher than those of monocultures and rotating crops on a regular basis. These methods relieve pressure on natural lands without reducing their overall productivity. No less important are social studies and educational programs that focus directly on the needs of the people who live on the land.

I have enough faith in human nature to believe that when people are both economically secure and aware of the value of biological wealth they will take the necessary measures to protect their environment. Out of that commitment will grow new knowledge and an enrichment of the human spirit beyond our present imagination.

The Growing Human Population

Development will stabilize populations, but will development come before population growth and harsh technologies do irremediable damage to the planet's life-support capacity?

. . .

Nathan Keyfitz

T he human life we know is set in a small space and in a small slice of time. If the earth were represented as a globe two feet in diameter, most life would be contained within the paint marking its surface, and the habitat of the five billion humans would be a thin layer within that. As recently as 10,000 years ago, people gathered into small Neolithic settlements. There were from five to 10 million human beings then—not enough to exercise much influence on the ecosystem within which they lived and worked. That situation prevailed for most of the next 10,000 years. Only in the past few decades have humans brought about changes comparable in magnitude to those wrought by nature during long epochs of geological time. Forests that grew over centuries and soils that took millions of years to develop are now being used up in a single human lifetime.

Figure 6.1 EXTREME CROWDING in Mexico City, the largest city in the world, forces millions of poor people to live in slums such as this one, where sewage disposal, adequate water supplies and other services do not exist. The city's population of 19.4 million is expected to swell to 24.4 million by the end of the century.

The population of the world at mid-century was 2.5 billion; some time in 1987 it passed five billion. The increase in the past 40 years has equaled the total increase over the millions of years from when the human species emerged until 1950. According to projections by the United Nations Population Division, the next 35 years (to 2025) will see a further increase to 8.5 billion (see Figure 6.2). Of the projected increase of some 3.2 billion, the United Nations finds that less than 200 million will be in the developed countries; at least three billion—that is, 95 percent—will be in the less developed countries.

Should we be worrying about the absolute increase of 3.2 billion people, or should we take satisfaction in the fact that the rate of increase is slowing? Between 1980 and 1985 total population increased by 9 percent; between 2020 and 2025 the increase is projected to be only 4 percent. Yet because the rate of increase applies to an ever larger base, the absolute population curve will continue upward. It will be well into the second quarter of the 21st century before the absolute number of births will come down even to the high levels of today. The population curve, of course, will continue to slope upward well beyond that time.

Is this progress or retrogression? Can one take satisfaction from the fact that the hungry will represent a declining fraction of the total population when their absolute number is increasing? Can one be glad that the rate of increase is slowing when it is not rates that wreak ecological destruction but absolute numbers of people?

The exponential growth of population and its attendant assault on the environment is so recent that it is difficult for people to appreciate how much damage is being done. Through long ages, many societies wanted more people; people added to the strength of the family and of the kingdom in which they labored. Death rates were so high that populations did not increase by much. The human population was viewed as a fragile entity in constant danger of extinction, locally if not globally. People were precious to their ruler, in much the same way as slaves were to their owners.

In 17th-century Europe the land could provide food for more people than were needed to work it. Hence, a ruler could put surplus laborers to work at the labor-intensive task of weaving cloth. The cloth could then be sold abroad in exchange for gold. That system was mercantilism, as practiced for example by Jean-Baptiste Colbert, finance minister to Louis XIV of France. Similar economic ideas were accepted throughout Europe. Even with the advent of machine production, large numbers of laborers could be employed, because although productivity per worker certainly increased, the demand for products increased even faster. Hence, labor remained a valued commodity.

Today rapid population growth is occurring simultaneously with improvements in production methods. In addition, an egalitarian ethos has spread in less developed countries as well as in industrialized ones. And so the conditions that prevailed until the 19th century—low population density on fertile land, labor-intensive technology and regard for the welfare of rulers rather than of workers—apply much less now. Labor-saving technology makes it more difficult to turn unequipped workers into gold. On the contrary, the less developed countries borrow capital to buy equipment in order to create employment for their people. Yet the equipment, designed in highly developed countries, requires relatively few hands to run it, and so even when borrowing by the less developed countries was at its height in the 1970's, unemployment kept increasing.

Are the unemployed evidence of overpopulation? Or are they not, rather, evidence of a badly run economy, in which the wages of those who do have jobs are kept artificially high? Anything, including labor, will remain unused if its price is maintained above what buyers can afford to pay for it. National leaders who see that it is politically impossible to free their labor markets at least want to add as few more people as possible, knowing that one birth prevented now is one unemployed person fewer in 2010 (see Figure 6.3). And since the same political forces are promoting the rapid spread of education, that unemployed person is likely to be a high school or college graduate and therefore especially dangerous to political stability.

Population increases, then, abetted by various aspects of technology and political structure, threaten social and political stability in the less developed countries. In addition, environmental issues are now emerging in the less developed as well as in the developed regions. One such issue is the flooding caused by deforestation; overlogging is directly related to the demand from ever-expanding populations for building material, firewood, additional farmland and foreign capital. Heavy floods caused by deforestation have recently led Thailand to ban all logging, and Malaysia is considering doing the same—even though both countries depend on timber and its products as an important source of employment and foreign exchange.

High birth rates in the countryside have forced many subsistence farmers onto marginal lands. In the Indian state of Rajasthan, arid soils are being rapidly depleted by intensive cultivation. The children of Javanese peasants, unable to make a living on subdivided plots of inherited land, have cleared mountainous terrain to grow crops, at the cost of much wasted labor and ecological damage. In Brazil peasants from overpopulated regions have destroyed millions of acres of rain forest in an attempt to eke out a living from soil that is essentially unsuitable for farming.

Meanwhile, more and more people are moving to cities, causing extraordinary urban concentration around the world. Before the advent of modern transport and the international grain trade, the size of a city was determined by its ability to command the agricultural surplus of farmland, usually in neighboring areas. All that has changed now: Mexico City (see Figure 6.1) and Caracas have grown by exchanging oil for food, New Delhi has grown by

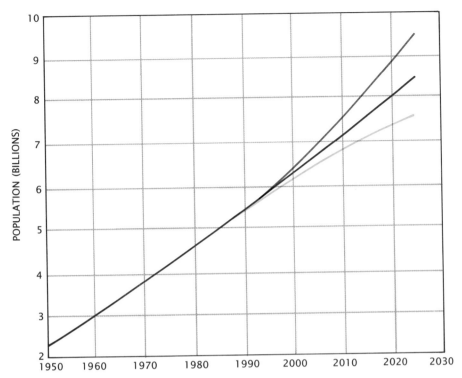

Figure 6.2 PROJECTIONS of the growing human population. If the growth rate were to remain near the current 1.74 percent a year until the year 2000 and decline thereafter to .98 percent in 2025, the world population will reach almost 8.5 billion in 2025 (*black*). If the growth rate were to decline at a faster rate and reach .59 percent by 2025, the population in 2025 will be around 7.6 billion (*blue*). If the growth rate were to climb to 1.9 percent at the end of the century before declining, the population in 2025 will be more than 9.4 billion (*red*). (Data supplied by U.N. Department of International Economic and Social Affairs.)

virtue of its political dominance and India's rail network, and Calcutta has grown by virtue of water transport. In cities that have nothing to exchange, foreign aid has intervened to mitigate hunger and so, incidentally, to increase population further.

No longer dependent on local products to trade for food and other necessities, cities around the world are expanding rapidly. A sixfold increase in urban population was foreseen for the world as a whole between 1950 and 2020. What is more, the growth of cities no longer has much relation to the level of development. Whereas only 17 percent of the population of the less developed countries was urban in 1950, well over 50 percent is expected to be urban in 2020.

From some points of view the concentration of people in cities has much to be said for it. To be sure, the air above Mexico City is scarcely

breathable—but this is a local effect. In spite of the bad air, city dwellers probably live longer than their country cousins. Certainly health care, education and other amenities are more easily provided to urban populations than to rural ones. When people are concentrated in cities, they would seem to have less direct effect on the forests, the wildlife, the oceans—on the biosphere in general.

A case might therefore be made for the ecological innocuousness of cities—were it not for one feature of modern urban dwellers: their unprecedented mobility. People in the middle class or higher, whether they live in developed or less developed countries, are mostly urban, and they are on the move incessantly—as commuters, as vacationers, for business or for pleasure, by car, bus and plane. And much of the damage to the ecosphere is related to movement and travel. A middle-class American eats

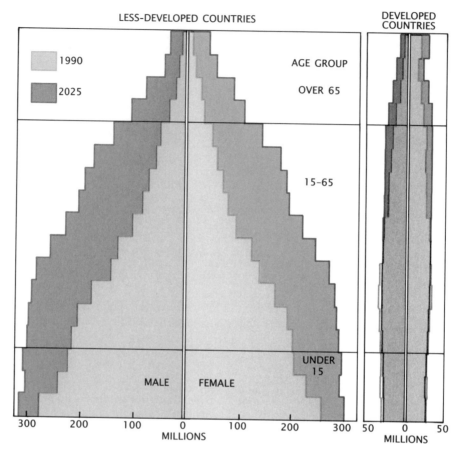

Figure 6.3 AGE DISTRIBUTION in less developed and developed countries in 1990 is compared with that projected for 2025. In less developed countries 37 percent of the population is under 15. Even if growth rates in these countries decline, populations will continue to grow rapidly when these young people reach childbearing age. The labor force will expand even faster than the total population of these countries; indeed, the number of working-age people in the world will triple between now and 2050. (Data furnished by U.N. Department of International Economic and Social Affairs.)

somewhat more than an Asian peasant, owns more clothes and has more varied entertainment, but none of these advantages requires extravagant amounts of resources. From an ecological perspective, it is the amount and mode of movement that principally distinguishes the American town dweller from the Asian peasant.

There are currently 500 million registered automobiles on the planet, and on the average they burn up nearly two gallons of fuel a day. Filling their tanks consumes about one third of the world's production of oil. Most of this feverish movement occurs among the 1.2 billion people in developed countries, but in the future most net growth in use of motor vehicles will take place in the less developed countries. Indeed, the number of automobiles is increasing more quickly than the population. At current rates of increase, by 2025 there will be four times as many automobiles as there are today.

The absolute increase in population, coupled with such trends as urbanization and greater mobility, clearly presents serious threats, especially for the less developed countries. Yet surely the absolute growth cannot continue forever. There must be some natural limit, some ultimate constraint. The 3.4 percent annual growth rate of Nigeria, for example, translates into a doubling of its population in 22 years. If Nigeria were to continue at this rate for the next 140 years, its population would be equal to that of the whole world today. Needless to say, this will not happen. Either its birth rate will fall or its death rate will rise. Because migration on a scale large enough to alleviate the pressure is out of the question, there are no other possibilities.

It is certain, then, that sooner or later growth has to stop. What are the natural limits, and what do they imply? Malthus assumed that the limit was food, but agricultural progress during the past two centuries has thrown that assumption into question (see Figure 6.4). Food surpluses exist in many nations, and even when famines do occur the cause is much · less the absence of food than its maldistribution—which is often accentuated by politics and civil war, as in the Sudan. Yet progress in agriculture does not exorcise other limits set by, for example, the availability of suitable living space, constraints on production and the limited capacity of the environment to absorb insults to it. To wait

for natural constraints to intervene to limit population size is to accept famine, low living standards, unemployment, political instability and ecological destruction. Society finds these options unacceptable. It must seek ways to curb population growth and to modify human activity so that it is environmentally more benign.

The first question, then, is two-pronged: How does a decline in growth come about, and how can progress toward this goal be accelerated? One of the most universally observed and least readily explained social phenomena of modern times is the demographic transition: the fact that with industrialization both death and birth rates fall to new low levels (see Figure 6.5). Medical advances are partly responsible for the fall in death rates; improvements in nutrition and other aspects of the way of life also play a considerable role. Because death rates drop first, populations experience large growth during the course of the transition: for example, Great Britain's population multiplied by four during the 19th century.

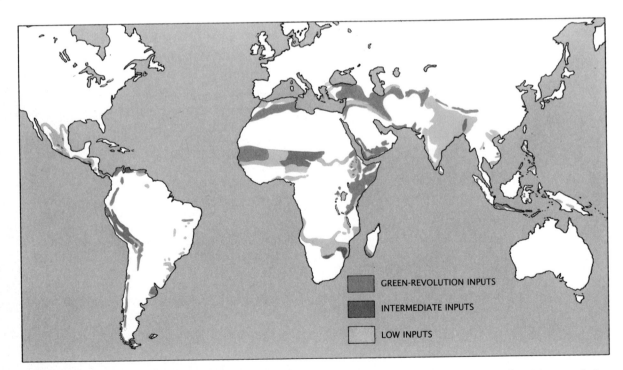

GREEN-REVOLUTION INPUTS

INTERMEDIATE INPUTS

LOW INPUTS

Figure 6.4 LOCAL FOOD PRODUCTION is outstripped by population in the shaded regions on this map. The assessments are based on local agricultural technology, where only traditional, low-input (low-capital) methods are available (*yellow*); where intermediate inputs are being are available (*yellow*); where intermediate inputs are being employed (*red*); and even where high, green-revolution inputs are being employed (*purple*).

Sooner or later after the fall of death rates, birth rates also start to decline. Indeed, birth rates do not merely drop to the point where they just offset the number of deaths (the condition that applied on the average throughout most of history); they fall below that, to the point where they fail to counterbalance deaths. The European countries, the U.S. and Japan have a disproportionately large number of people of childbearing age because of high fertility in the recent past. Consequently, they will continue to grow for some time. Once the current generation has passed, however, the populations of these countries could fall by anywhere from one tenth to one third in each generation.

In analyzing the demographic transition, what requires explanation—the low birth rates of the present or the high birth rates of the past? One view is that people have always wanted to be relieved of the burden of child rearing but did not have convenient (or effective) methods of birth control. Another is that children were desired because they provided security in old age, as well as extra hands and marriage ties to other families. Wives were subordinate to husbands, and whatever else the wife was doing, the husband could set her to childbearing as well. This behavior pattern was inculcated into boys and girls from earliest childhood, and the whole structure was supported by pronatalist doctrine, in particular of religion.

Yet religious doctrine by itself is less than decisive for determining fertility: witness the recent decline in birth rates in some of the most developed Catholic societies, such as Italy, Austria and the province of Quebec. Apparently some other elements of culture offset religious influence on birth rates as countries develop. One prominent social factor is the improved status of women. For example, in regions such as Java, where women enjoy greater rights and better education than they do in other Muslim regions, birth rates are falling, whereas in Muslim regions such as Pakistan, Bangladesh and certain Arab countries, where women have low status, birth rates remain high.

Modern industry and commerce make it possible for women to earn their own income and become financially independent of their husbands. Similarly, children enter the work force and become independent of their parents, and parents become independent of their children to the extent that they can rely on social security and private savings. If a child is no longer a source of economic support, will the effort of raising children seem worthwhile? If one knew what mechanisms led to the drop in birth rates, the industrialized nations could check their failure to reproduce and the poor nations would know how to bring their birth rates down.

Whatever the mechanisms, it is certain that birth rates in the less developed countries will decline as the countries develop. Their economic development is hindered by large and growing populations, however, and so the scale of development will have to be enormous in order for the benefits to reach everyone. The strain on the environment will therefore be unprecedented. Brazil says it cannot develop without cutting down Amazon forests, and it resents foreign demands for restraint. Population growth in some areas is now so great that the limits of materials and the environment have already been reached; this strain has slowed the economic development that would check births. In the face of such a danger, the urgency of birth-control programs cannot be stressed enough.

Regardless of the deeper origins of low birth rates, abundant evidence shows that information about birth control and access to contraceptives have been major causes of declining fertility in all countries. In Asian nations that established family-planning programs in the 1960's—China, Indonesia, Thailand and South Korea—crude birth rates declined by from 25 to 60 percent over two decades. In Tunisia birth rates dropped about twice as fast in the decade after the program began as in the previous seven years. The birth rate in Mauritius was nearly 40 per 1,000 before 1965, when a birth-control program was initiated, and it dropped to below 25 per 1,000 during the first eight years of the program. Mexico set up a program in 1973, and its birth rate fell within about four years from some 45 per 1,000 to some 38; the rate is currently about 31 per 1,000.

Policymakers would like to know how much of these declines can be attributed to the programs and how much would have occurred in any case because of general socioeconomic improvements (see Figure 6.6). Using data from 19 developing countries, Timothy King of the World Bank has calculated that family-planning programs account for 39 percent of the decline and overall socioeconomic improvement for 54 percent. Other investigators, who used different data but applied essentially the same method, report that family-planning programs account for from 10 to 40 percent of observed de-

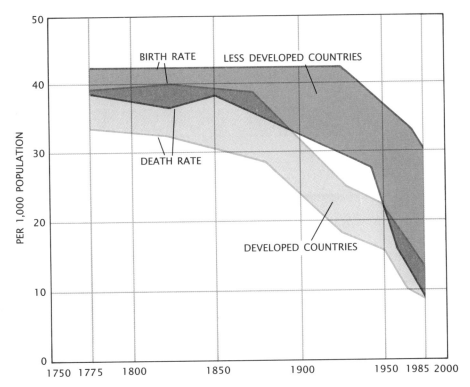

Figure 6.5 INDUSTRIALIZATION in the developed regions led to a fall in death rates, followed by a drop in birth rates that began a little over a century ago. Having passed through this "demographic transition," the developed regions now have a net growth (*shaded area*) of only about .4 percent. In contrast, the decline in death rates in the less developed countries has not yet been compensated by the decline in birth rates.

clines in birth rates; no serious study has failed to find some effect. It is worth noting that the first stages of modernization often lead to temporary increases in fertility, because traditional methods of birth control—extended breast-feeding and postpartum abstinence—are typically abandoned. Hence, the actual effect of family-planning programs is considerably greater than the initial figures indicate.

Indonesia's family-planning program began officially in 1970. By 1980 the National Family Planning Coordinating Board had established more than 40,000 village distribution centers for contraceptive devices and information, mostly in Java and Bali. These centers are often linked to agricultural cooperatives and health services and so become intrinsic aspects of the country's development efforts. They provide social centers where people receive free contraceptives. Educational programs promote the notion that a family should be "small, happy and prosperous" (see Figure 6.7). The barrage of public messages about family planning is relentless: the national family-planning jingle plays when a train passes a railway crossing, religious leaders give lectures on contraception at the local mosque (Islam accepts birth control, with the exception of permanent sterilization), and at five o'clock every afternoon sirens wail to remind women to take their pill.

Indonesia's campaign has met with notable success. Since 1972 the fertility rate has fallen from 5.6 to 3.4 children per woman; whereas 400,000 couples practiced birth control in 1972, in 1989 more than 18.6 million couples did so. Infant mortality meanwhile has fallen by 40 percent. It is interesting that abortion is illegal in Indonesia; the lowering of the birth rate was brought about by strong government and community support, education—and the dissemination of free contraceptives to any couple who wanted them. The country's family-planning strategists hope eventually to get couples—those

SOCIO-ECONOMIC SETTING	1982 FAMILY-PLANNING PROGRAM STRENGTH				MEAN
	STRONG	MODERATE	WEAK	VERY WEAK OR NONE	
	COUNTRY PERCENT	COUNTRY PERCENT	COUNTRY PERCENT	COUNTRY PERCENT	
HIGH	HONG KONG 80 SINGAPORE 71 TAIWAN 70 KOREA 58 COLOMBIA 51 MEXICO 40	CUBA 79 PANAMA 63 JAMAICA 55 TRINIDAD/TOBAGO 54 FIJI 38	COSTA RICA 66 BRAZIL 50 VENEZUELA 49 PERU 43 CHILE 43	PARAGUAY 36	
MEAN	60	58	50	36	55
UPPER MIDDLE	CHINA 69 SRI LANKA 57	THAILAND 58 PHILIPPINES 45 DOMINICAN REPUBLIC 43 MALAYSIA 42 EL SALVADOR 34 TUNISIA 31	ECUADOR 40 TURKEY 40 HONDURAS 27 EGYPT 24 MOROCCO 19 GUATEMALA 18 ALGERIA 7	IRAN 23 SYRIA 20 GHANA 10 NICARAGUA 9 ZAIRE 3 ZAMBIA 1	
MEAN	63	42	25	11	30
LOWER MIDDLE	INDONESIA 48	INDIA 32 VIETNAM 21	HAITI 19 ZIMBABWE 14 KENYA 7 PAKISTAN 6 PAPUA NEW GUINEA 5 SENEGAL 4 LIBERIA 1	BOLIVIA 24 NIGERIA 6 LESOTHO 6 BURMA 7 CAMEROON 2 UGANDA 1 KAMPUCHEA 0	
MEAN	48	27	8	6	12
LOW		BANGLADESH 19	NEPAL 7 TANZANIA 1	BENIN 18 SUDAN 5 SIERRA LEONE 4 ETHIOPIA 2 SOMALIA 2 YEMEN 1 BURUNDI 1 CHAD 1 GUINEA 1 MALAWI 1 MALI 1 NIGER 1 BURKINA FASO 1 MAURITANIA	
MEAN		19	4	3	4
MEAN	59	44	23	7	26

Figure 6.6 EFFECTIVENESS of family-planning programs is shown by measuring the percentage of couples who use contraceptives in less developed countries. Given comparable socioeconomic settings, the percentage of couples who use contraceptives is higher in countries that have stronger programs than in countries with weaker programs. The study was carried out by the late Robert J. Lapham of Demographic and Health Surveys and W. Parker Mauldin of the Rockefeller Foundation.

who can afford it—to pay for their contraceptives: they want people to take responsibility for family planning and to consider contraceptives a commodity worth paying for.

It is especially important to give couples the widest possible choice of contraceptive methods. The contraceptive pill and condoms require effective distribution systems to ensure that couples have a constant supply. Intrauterine devices and injections of Depo-Provera (a synthetic hormone) are more convenient in that they only require occasional visits to health clinics (see Figure 6.8). All these methods have possible side effects, however, ranging from irregular menstrual bleeding to pelvic infections, which can discourage women from adopting a method and sticking to it. Among the more recent and most promising developments are contraceptives such as Norplant that can be implanted under the skin and are effective for up to five years. Still, there remains a great need for safer, more convenient and inexpensive birth-control methods.

For some of the countries of Asia and especially of Africa, the pronatalist culture is too strong for family-planning programs to have much effect. Programs set up in Pakistan, Nepal and Kenya have had little success. Family-planning programs can

Figure 6.7 INDONESIAN INFANT is weighed as his mother looks on. The country's infant-health program sponsors monthly weighings, which enable mothers to monitor the development of their children. The program subtly promotes the idea that parents with small families are better able to care for their children.

work only if countries are economically and socially ready to accept them. Based on a series of surveys conducted under the auspices of the World Fertility Survey, most of the less developed countries are now at the point where sizable portions of their populations want smaller families than has tradi-

tionally been the norm. This finding, at least, is cause for optimism.

The impact of people depends not only on their number but also on their setting in the biosphere and on their economic activities. Can

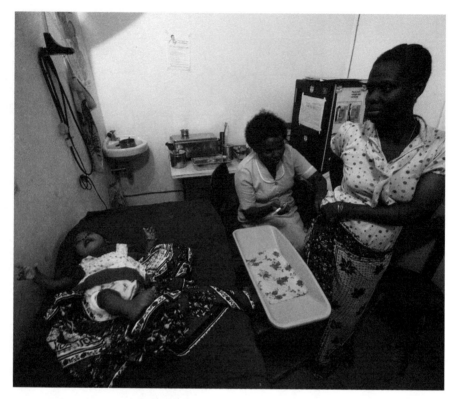

Figure 6.8 KENYAN WOMAN receives an injection of the contraceptive Depo-Provera at a health clinic. She and her husband already have four children; the youngest lies on the table. "If we have more, how can we send them to school, how can we feed them?" she asks. The Kenyan government has recently begun to discuss instituting family-planning programs, a major change from past policy. At its current annual growth rate of more than 4 percent, Kenya's population of 25.1 million will double in 17 years.

changes in economic practices rather than in population growth mitigate the harmful effects on the environment? In Europe, North America and much of Asia, the traditional culture has usually taken a long-range perspective on its impact on the environment: good traditional farming and forestry practices entailed maintaining the land in such condition that it would keep producing indefinitely.

But tradition is not everywhere a protection: the loggers of Nepal and the cattle raisers of the Sahel have traditions that—under the pressure of growing populations—are improvident. One could say of them, as of many other societies, that if they were fewer in number, they would destroy less; if they had better practices, they would destroy less. If there were fewer people to drive automobiles, less fuel would be consumed and less smog generated; if people relied on public transport, the results would be similarly beneficial.

A purely cultural feature underlies the economics. One can demonstrate this by noting that an Austrian town may have its own swimming pool and that hundreds of people walk to it on weekends, doing essentially the same thing as their American counterparts do by driving 100 miles or so to go to a beach. For affluent people everywhere, the urge to get into one's car and drive 100 miles or to board a jet and fly across the country to swim and sunbathe is strong. Will the culture shift in a direction that will spare the biosphere? That question is as hard to answer for American sunbathers as it is for African cattle herders.

Everywhere there is this symmetry between numbers of people on the one hand and harmful practices on the other. Hence, the endless debate on appropriate policies. Some argue that the number of people does little harm in itself but only exacerbates the effect of bad practices; others argue that bad

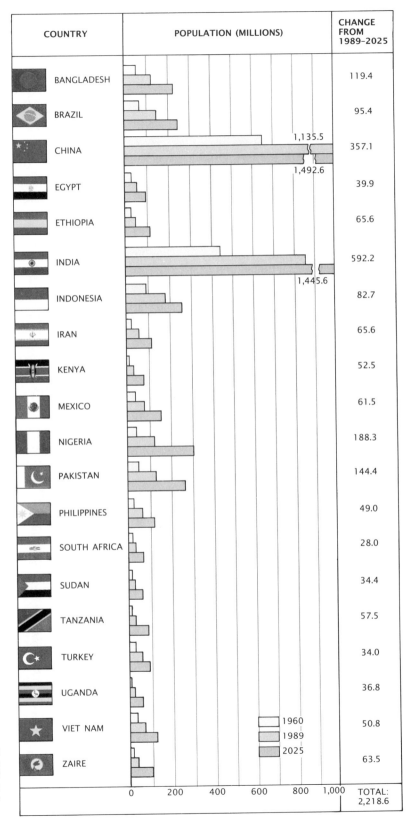

COUNTRY	POPULATION (MILLIONS)	CHANGE FROM 1989–2025
BANGLADESH		119.4
BRAZIL		95.4
CHINA	1,135.5 / 1,492.6	357.1
EGYPT		39.9
ETHIOPIA		65.6
INDIA	1,445.6	592.2
INDONESIA		82.7
IRAN		65.6
KENYA		52.5
MEXICO		61.5
NIGERIA		188.3
PAKISTAN		144.4
PHILIPPINES		49.0
SOUTH AFRICA		28.0
SUDAN		34.4
TANZANIA		57.5
TURKEY		34.0
UGANDA		36.8
VIET NAM		50.8
ZAIRE		63.5
	0 200 400 600 800 1,000	TOTAL: 2,218.6

1960
1989
2025

Figure 6.9 SEVENTY PERCENT of the projected increase in world population by the year 2025 will occur in these 20 less developed countries. (Data from U.N. Department of International Economic and Social Affairs.)

practices should of course be rectified but meanwhile the size of the population should be controlled.

What are the population-policy questions regarding the assault on the planet? They will involve the relation between population and agricultural and industrial technology and will have to be dealt with in the context of conflicts between less developed and developed countries and of civil and international wars in the less developed countries. The path of development will be rough for the people concerned—and in many places the degree of difficulty will be in proportion to the size of the population.

People ultimately will become aware of how their own childbearing affects the future ecological stability of their country and of the planet. If the ecological base of an economy is undermined by overpopulation, this cannot but depress economic growth. People will come to understand that it is preferable to have a few children of high quality rather than to have many children who will be uneducated and unemployed. Good policies will make expensive to citizens that which is expensive to the nation. The ecological (and other) costs of children to the community must be transmitted to the individual parents. Yet no one wants to tax excessive childbearing in such a way as to harm the children who are already born. This concern makes it much more difficult to fashion effective family policy than it is to, say, develop commodity-consumption policies.

All these concerns apply particularly to the less developed countries, where almost all the future increases in world population will occur (see Figure 6.9). Some experts are concerned that population growth in the developed nations will soon cease entirely and urge action to counter this possibility. Stimulating growth in the more developed countries, however, would set a bad example and, worse, would seem to carry a racist message: there are too many of you and not enough of us.

But the developed nations can do more for the planet and for economic development than merely set a good example on population control. They can become more aware of how their policies affect the less developed countries. They cannot expect to collect debts from developing nations without accepting their exports. By imposing tariffs against export items in the less developed regions and insisting on debt repayment, the developed nations undermine the ability of the less developed regions to sustain their populations.

Certain agricultural and forestry goods, such as Senegal's peanuts and Thailand's plywood, are important means by which these countries earn foreign exchange, but these products can exact a high ecological cost. The subsidies that stimulate European and American farmers to produce surplus food have an unnecessarily deleterious effect on the environment. Shipping excess wheat and corn to the less developed countries is a desirable form of charity to relieve a food emergency, but not when the foreign grains discourage local agriculture.

Even with some care in management, industrial development pollutes air and water and is destructive in other ways. Education will increase awareness of these destructive effects and lower the birth rate; hence, it will ultimately lessen the stress on the environment. A sufficient level of economic development should bring a corresponding mastery of all problems, including ecological ones. Yet if the environment is mishandled badly enough, that in itself will slow down or even prevent further development.

The question each country must face, then, is how to attain a sufficient pace of economic development without destroying the environment: that eventuality would make any future economic advances impossible. Most less developed nations are aware that the pace of development would be faster and the destruction of the environment slower if their populations were to increase more slowly than they do today. Not all of them have the same capacity to formulate and implement policies that will put that knowledge to use.

Strategies for Agriculture

Agricultural research will probably yield many new technologies for expanding food production while preserving land, water and genetic diversity. The real trick will be getting farmers to use them.

. . .

Pierre R. Crosson and Norman J. Rosenberg

One hundred years from now the earth may have 10 billion inhabitants, about twice as many as it has now. If projections made by demographers at the World Bank are correct, the human population will by then be approaching a stable level, as the populations of many industrialized countries already have. Will our species be able to feed itself when this steady state is reached? The short answer is probably yes. World food production could grow significantly more slowly than the current rate, and there would still be enough food for 10 billion mouths by the time they arrive (see Figure 7.2).

The long answer is not quite as simple. Not only must the food supply expand, it must expand in a way that does not destroy the natural environment. For that to happen, a steady stream of new technologies that minimize erosion, desertification, salinization of the soil and other environmental damage must be introduced. We are confident that if the strong system of agricultural-research organizations already in place is provided with enough financial support and leadership, it will develop these techniques. But we also believe that developing new technology is not the most difficult problem facing the world's agriculture; society is.

In order for new, less damaging techniques to have an effect, they must be used. For them to be introduced at the level of the individual farm, they must benefit the farmer. In a market system, such benefit generally takes the form of profit. Yet markets are not well equipped to protect resources such as water and genetic diversity, in which it is difficult to establish property rights. In our view the most challenging problem for agricultural policy is to devise institutional mechanisms that will reward individual farmers for valuing these precious resources at their true social worth.

The pressure to develop new agricultural technologies will be roughly proportional to the rate of depletion of natural resources employed in agriculture. Of these resources, three—land, water and genetic diversity—are critical, and those are the three we shall focus on in this article.

In many parts of the world the supply of agricultural land is threatened by various kinds of degradation. Among the most important forms are erosion by wind and water and the consequent loss of soil productivity; degradation of rangelands in the arid, semiarid and subhumid regions; and waterlogging and salinization of irrigated lands. All these

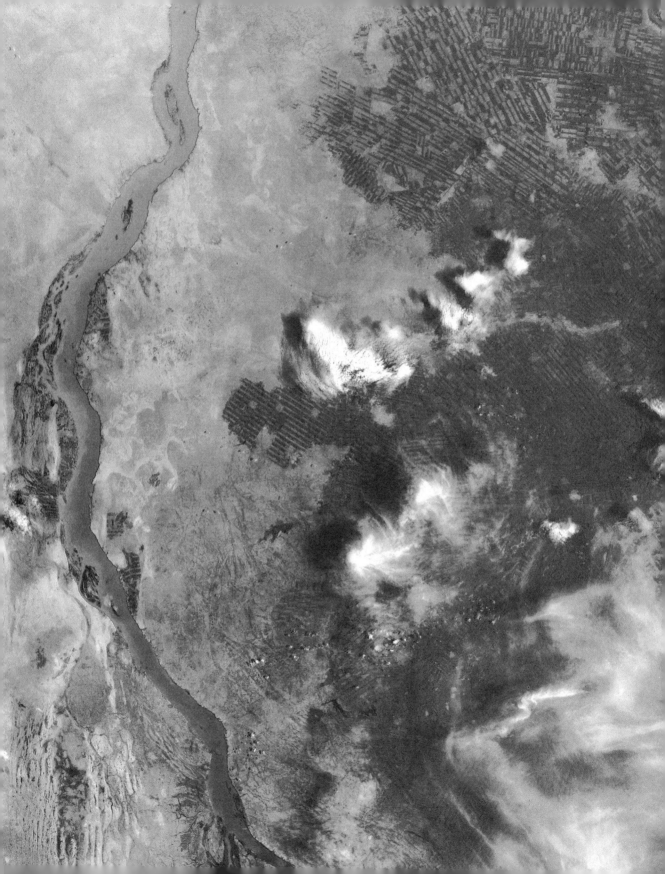

processes can be considered under the general heading of desertification (even though that term in the popular imagination suggests only the expansion of desert onto adjacent rangeland or farmland), and that is the rubric under which they will be treated here.

Data compiled by the United Nations Environment Program (UNEP) indicate that about 60 percent of the 3.3 billion hectares of agricultural land that are not in humid regions is affected to some degree by desertification as broadly defined above. (One hectare is 2.47 acres.) Such a large fraction suggests desertification is a major problem in the world today.

Yet all such global estimates must be taken with more than a few grains of salt. For one thing, they depend on the definition of desertification, which may vary. For another, in most of the world's regions accurate estimates of degradative processes are not available. Take the case of erosion. The U.S. is the only country in the world that has reasonably accurate and comprehensive estimates of soil erosion and its effect on productivity. Those estimates suggest that if current rates of cropland erosion prevail for 100 years, crop yields will be from 3 to 10 percent lower than they would be otherwise. Yield increases (resulting from technology) that are modest by historical standards would much more than compensate for such a loss.

Estimates of erosion have been made for other parts of the world—some showing very large losses. But experts who have examined these estimates closely, including a review carried out for the United Nations Food and Agriculture Organization in 1984, concluded that these evaluations have little scientific merit. There is no question that erosion and the resulting loss of productivity is significant in some regions, including Nepal, parts of India, the highlands of East Africa and parts of the Andes. The importance of these losses in relation to the world's total output of food, however, is quite uncertain, and apocalyptic scenarios ought to be evaluated skeptically.

Even areas that have been subject to desertification are not necessarily lost to agriculture forever. The overwhelming share of the land reported to the UNEP as desertified is rangeland. Rangeland is subject to degradation around the world, but events in the Sahelian zone of Africa provide a striking example. Rapid growth of population in the Sahel and the Horn of Africa after World War II led to an increase in grazing pressure that would by itself have led to a decline in range productivity. The process of degradation was intensified by a severe drought that began in the 1960's and has continued intermittently since.

Yet satellite images show that even the depleted Sahelian rangeland and farmland can recuperate. In years of good rainfall the so-called Green Wave of vegetation extends farther north into the Sahel than it does during dry years (see Figure 7.3). It is likely that high-quality vegetation does not return immediately to the overgrazed areas, but it does seem that with carefully controlled grazing programs in place much apparently desertified land could recover. The problem, of course, is to maintain "careful control" where the population is growing rapidly and there is a tradition of unhindered access to the land. As we shall argue later on, the chief difficulties facing world agriculture stem from the lack of institutions for handling such situations and not from inexorable natural processes.

Another aspect of desertification, broadly defined, is salinization. In areas where irrigation water contains large quantities of dissolved salts, improper irrigation practices and lack of drainage often lead to salt buildup in the soil and direct damage to growing plants. According to James D. Rhoades of the U.S. Salinity Laboratory in Riverside, Calif., irrigation water can contain as much as 3.5 tons of salt per 1,000 cubic meters. Since crops often require from 6,000 to 9,500 cubic meters of water per hectare each year, that amount of land may receive up to 33 tons of salt. Little of the salt is taken up by plants; most of it is left behind in the soil as the water evaporates.

Technical means for dealing with salinization are known: the salt must be flushed out of the root zone by applying excess water. Yet when this is done, the problem is often only moved on. If drainage water reenters the supplying canal, the salt content of the irrigation water is increased for all users farther downstream. The key problem in reducing salinization is the absence of institutions and policies that

Figure 7.1 IRRIGATED CROPLAND appears red in this satellite photograph made over the Nile where it flows through the Sudan. In the past 70 years, a variety of irrigation projects have increased the agricultural productivity of this dry region. More than half of the increase in the world's agricultural productivity during the past few decades has come from irrigation.

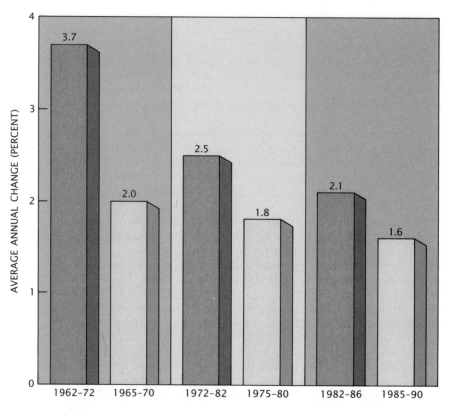

Figure 7.2 WORLD FOOD PRODUCTION is growing faster than population. The chart shows the annual increase in total production of cereals (*red*) and in the world's population (*blue*). If the food supply can be increased at the current pace (or even a slower one), there will be enough food for a stable world population of 10 billion in 100 years.

require the upstream farmer to take account of the consequences of his actions for those downstream.

The conversion of rural land to urban uses is an inevitable part of economic development; sometimes it is seen as a threat to the supply of land for agricultural production. In the 1970's a study by the U.S. Department of Agriculture and the Council on Environmental Quality concluded that by the 1990's the conversion of agricultural land could present the nation with a resource-scarcity problem as serious as the then prevailing energy crisis. Subsequent analysis has greatly diminished such concern, and the issue is no longer much discussed in the U.S.

In countries where farmland is less abundant than it is in the U.S. (in Asia, for example), urbanization may be a larger threat. Yet some data suggest that even in Asia the problem is not yet very imposing. In northern India (where about half of the country's people live) and in Bangladesh, both cropland and urban land increased from 1950 to 1980. (The reason both can increase is that areas in neither category, such as forested regions, may be converted to urban or agricultural purposes.) In India in 1980 urban land included about a tenth as much area as cropland did; in Bangladesh the fraction was about an eighth. Hence, even in these crowded countries, a rapid increase in the amount of urban land would reduce the amount of cropland by relatively little.

In addition to land, the other natural resources central to agriculture are water and genetic diversity. Water is particularly important: data gathered by the World Bank indicate that the spread of irrigation contributed between 50 and 60 percent of the massive increase in agricultural output of the developing countries from 1960 to 1980 (see Figure 7.1).

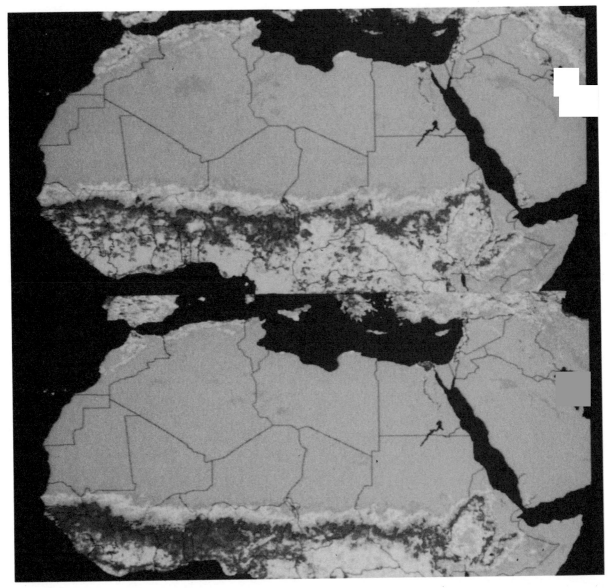

Figure 7.3 "GREEN WAVE" appears each year as vegetation is revived by seasonal rains moving north into the Sahelian zone south of the Sahara. These maps were generated by computer treatment of satellite data. Vegetation is shown on a scale extending from tan (little or no vegetation) through purple (heavy vegetation). In 1980 (*upper map*), a year of "ordinary" rainfall, the Green Wave extended farther than in 1984 (*lower map*), when the rains were disastrously low. An extended drought and overgrazing have made the Sahel a heavily "desertified" region, but even there the process is reversible, as the maps suggest.

Although there is still potential for expanded irrigation, such expansion will be more expensive than it has been in the past, because low-cost sources of water were exploited first.

Furthermore, demographic and economic growth steadily increase the competition for water—a competition in which agriculture does not fare well, since the return on investments in water is generally lower in agriculture than in urban or industrial uses. In addition, in some parts of the developing world, the supply of water for irrigation is also threatened by the buildup of silt in reservoirs. Reservoirs are designed to accept a certain amount of silt, but in some areas deforestation, overgrazing and erosive cropping practices are causing reservoirs to be filled much faster than at the designed rate. Although the evidence is anecdotal, it suggests that siltation is not a trivial threat.

The threat to genetic diversity in agriculture is somewhat more difficult to determine. Since World War II there has been a worldwide trend away from crop rotation and toward continuous raising of a single crop, such as corn. Monocropping can lead to sharp reductions in genetic diversity, with ominous results. A striking example occurred in the U.S. in 1970, when corn production was reduced 15 percent by a fungus well matched to the "T-cytoplasm" that had been incorporated in most of the hybrid seed corn planted in the U.S. corn belt. By the following year seed producers had stopped relying on the T-cytoplasm, and a more variable genetic basis was reestablished.

Up to this point we have considered the natural resources that are crucial for the continuing growth of agricultural production. But it is also clear that agricultural growth has potent consequences for the environment in general. Some of these processes are taken up in greater detail elsewhere in this book. Clearing forestland to plant crops reduces the variety of vegetation and has adverse effects on animal habitat. In tropical rain forests such effects may be severe (see Chapter 5, "Threats to Biodiversity," by Edward O. Wilson). Several radiatively active trace gases released by agricultural processes, including carbon dioxide, methane and nitrous oxide, contribute to the greenhouse effect (see Chapter 3, "The Changing Climate," by Stephen H. Schneider).

Of course, the greenhouse effect and the loss of animal habitat are not the result of agriculture alone. Some threats to the environment, however, are specific to agriculture, and among these is the increasing burden of pesticides and fertilizers. Pesticides and fertilizers are, along with irrigation and higher-yielding crop varieties, responsible for much of the remarkable increase in agricultural productivity that has taken place in the past few decades (see Figure 7.4). But these substances can also have unfortunate side effects. Fertilizers and pesticides in groundwater may cause ailments ranging from cancer to methemoglobinemia ("blue baby syndrome"), which results from excess concentrations of nitrates in drinking water. Although good data are lacking, the rapid increase in the use of these

agents around the world undoubtedly has some fairly serious health implications.

As the preceding paragraphs suggest, the challenge to agriculture is not only to provide food for the 10 billion people who will probably be living a century from now but also to achieve that level of production with less environmental damage than is apparent today. This twofold goal is often discussed under the heading of "sustainable agriculture." Achieving sustainability will clearly require continued long-term support for nationally based agricultural-research establishments and for the 13 institutes in the Consultative Group on International Agricultural Research (CGIAR), headquartered at the World Bank in Washington, D.C. (see Figure 7.5).

The CGIAR system is a major resource for research on new agricultural technologies for developing countries. Indeed, the Green Revolution of the 1960's was largely the result of varieties of rice and wheat developed by research workers at CGIAR institutes in the Philippines and in Mexico (see Figure 7.6). The Green Revolution in turn was a major component of the increase in world food production that has taken place in recent decades. The World Resources Institute has estimated that from the mid-1960's to the mid-1980's world food production increased at an annual rate of 2.4 percent. Grain production grew even faster: at an annual rate of 2.9 percent.

These substantial increases, combined with the fact that the growth rate of the world's population has recently slowed to less than 2 percent (see Chapter 6, "The Growing Human Population," by Nathan Keyfitz), provide the basis for our optimism that food production will keep pace with population growth. Meeting that goal sustainably, however, will necessitate a steady stream of new agricultural technologies that can only come from the CGIAR system and national research institutions in both the developed and the developing countries. What technologies are needed? Although one might point to any number of innovations, three categories seem of particular importance: those that reduce the environmental burden of pesticides and fertilizers, those that reduce the demand for irrigation water and those that continue to improve crop production per hectare.

One of the main components of fertilizer is nitrogen. If plants other than legumes could be biologically engineered so as to "fix" nitrogen in the soil, the demand for fertilizer would be greatly reduced. A prime candidate for such a transformation is corn.

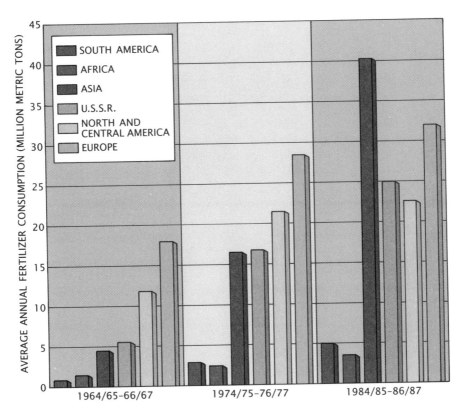

Figure 7.4 USE OF FERTILIZER serves as one measure of the burden agriculture places on the environment. The chart shows the total quantity of fertilizer that is employed in the world's major regions. In most regions fertilizer use has increased sharply in recent years. Comprehensive data on the remainder of the global environmental burden from agriculture (including pesticide production) are not available.

The job will clearly require the resources of biotechnology, which make it possible to manipulate the genetic material of an organism directly. Biotechnology has already proved its worth in a number of applications related to animal production, and the engineering of a nitrogen-fixing corn is by no means out of reach. Indeed, Frederick Ausubel of the Harvard Medical School noted recently that "it is simply an extremely complex engineering job" that will almost certainly be accomplished within 50 years.

Both old and new techniques are now being put to the task of saving irrigation water. "Water harvesting," a technique employed in the Middle East in pre-Christian times, calls for the land to be shaped to permit rain to run off large upland areas into collection devices or to spread out over smaller areas in sufficient quantities to wet the root zone fully. The efficiency of gravity-flow irrigation systems made up of basins and furrows, probably the most widely used type, can be improved by a high-tech method: laser leveling. Lasers can be employed to guide machines that level growing fields, making it possible to flood them quickly and uniformly.

Another system—trickle, or drip, irrigation—depends on a higher overall level of technology than gravity-fed systems. Trickle irrigation gained wide acceptance in Israel, the U.S. and other countries in the 1970's and is now being introduced around the world. Trickle systems deliver water directly to a small area adjacent to an individual plant. The water is carried by tubing, generally plastic, that may be either buried or placed on the surface; usually a nozzle called an "emitter" releases the water at the appropriate location.

Trickle systems, along with some others, not only increase efficiency in the use of irrigation water but also offer new approaches to preventing salinization. One new strategy emphasizes keeping salts (and other pollutants such as pesticides) on the land

Center	Year Established	Location	Mandate
Centro Internacional de Agricultura Tropical	1966	Cali, Colombia	Improve production of beans, cassava, rice, and beef in the Tropics of the Western Hemisphere
Centro Internacional de la Papa	1971	Lima, Peru	Improve the potato in the Andes and develop new varieties for lower tropics
Centro Internacional de Mejoramiento de Maiz y Trigo	1943 1966	Mexico City	Improve maize, wheat, barley, and triticale
International Board for Plant Genetic Resources	1974	Rome, Italy	Promote an international network of genetic-resources (germplasm) centers
International Center for Agricultural Research in the Dry Areas	1977	Aleppo, Syria	Focus on rainfed agriculture in arid and semiarid regions in North Africa and West Asia
International Crops Research Institute for the Semi-Arid Tropics	1972	Andhra Pradesh, India	Improve quantity and reliability of food production in the semiarid tropics
International Food Policy Research Institute	1974	Washington, D.C.	Address issues arising from governmental and international agency intervention in national, regional, and global food problems
International Institute of Tropical Agriculture	1967	Ibadan, Nigeria	Be responsible for improvement of worldwide cowpea, yarn, cocoyam, and sweet potato, and for cassava, rice, maize, beans, among others
International Laboratory for Research on Animal Disease	1974	Nairobi, Kenya	Help develop controls for trypanosomiasis (transmitted by the tsetse fly) and theileriosis (transmitted by ticks)
International Livestock Centre for Africa	1974	Addis Ababa, Ethiopia	Conduct research and development on improved livestock production and marketing systems, train livestock specialists, and gather documentation for livestock industry
International Rice Research Institute	1960	Los Banos, Philippines	Select and breed improved rice varieties, maintain a germplasm collection bank
International Service for National Agricultural Research	1980	The Hague, The Netherlands	Strengthen national agricultural research systems
West Africa Development Association	1971	Monrovia, Liberia	Promote self-sufficiency in rice in West Africa and improve varieties suitable for the area's agroclimate and socioeconomic conditions

Figure 7.5 CGIAR SYSTEM, the Consultative Group on International Agricultural Research, consists of 13 agricultural-research institutions. Each has a specific mandate. New strains of rice and wheat developed in the CGIAR system were largely responsible for the Green Revolution that greatly boosted agricultural productivity in the developing countries during the 1960's.

rather than passing them back into the water supply. This is done by cycling wastewater back into the farm's irrigation system and strategically reapplying it to the fields at times and in ways that minimize the effects of the salts carried in it.

Trickle irrigation is particularly helpful in this regard. Much of the damage to crops from salt comes from the salt left behind after water is supplied and then evaporates repeatedly. High concentrations of salt outside the roots of plants lower the osmotic pressure and make it more difficult for the plant to take water in from the surrounding soil. In trickle systems, however, plant roots are continuously supplied with water, and the salts do not build up enough to make water uptake difficult.

Another group of agricultural innovations entails not specific high-tech solutions but the application of (sometimes ancient) principles of integration to crops. The concept of multiple cropping takes in crop rotations, intercropping (sometimes with trees and annual crops sharing the same field), overseeding legumes into cereals and also double cropping —growing two or more crops simultaneously in a single field. Multiple cropping is an old tradition. For example, a system employed in Central America since pre-Columbian times calls for growing maize, beans and squash together. The maize provides a trellis for the beans; the beans enrich the soil with nitrogen; the squash provides ground cover, reducing erosion, soil compaction and weed growth.

Trees can be used in multiple cropping systems. In Europe, North Africa, the U.S.S.R. and the Great Plains regions of Canada and the U.S., windbreaks (see Figure 7.7) made up of trees protect growing crops from mechanical damage and the drying effect of wind. Elsewhere, shade trees grow in combination with shade-loving plants such as coffee, annual crops such as maize or beans, or pasture. The trees provide fodder, erosion control and fuel. In West Africa leaf litter from *Acacia alba* trees enriches the soil for the benefit of various grain and vegetable crops grown between them.

In addition to its ecological advantages, multiple cropping can sharply increase crop yields. In the American Midwest farmers are experimentally growing corn with other, low-growing plants. In

Figure 7.6 NEW STRAINS OF RICE grow on a Philippine hillside near the International Rice Research Institute (IRRI) at Los Banos. High-yielding, pest-resistant varieties of rice developed at IRRI have greatly increased the yield in rice-producing regions of Asia.

one experiment in an irrigated field in western Nebraska, two-row corn windbreaks were spaced every 15 rows throughout a field of sugar beets. The wind shelter provided by the corn increased the yield of sugar by 11 percent. The greater sunlight penetration and more rapid replenishment of carbon dioxide to the corn's leaves increased the yield of corn by 150 percent.

Multiple cropping has another important advantage. In fields where crops are rotated regularly, pests, including weeds, insects and pathogens, cannot adapt themselves to a single set of environmental conditions and therefore do not increase as quickly. Where two types of crops are grown in a single field, the pests in one type are sometimes kept down by predators that inhabit the other. Such beneficial interactions can be consciously employed to form the basis of a method called integrated pest management (IPM).

IPM includes the use of a wide range of techniques—chemical pest control, mechanical manipulation of the soil and many biological strategies—to control pests while minimizing the environmental burden of chemicals and frequent passages of tillage and pest-control machinery through the fields. A good example comes from the cotton-growing regions of Texas. IPM in Texas has several aspects: choice of cotton varieties that mature early (throwing them out of synchrony with the typical cotton pests), encouragement of the predators that consume pests such as the boll weevil and the bollworm, and the burning of all plant residues after the harvest, a practice that destroys many larvae. This system works well on cotton in Texas. Yet it should be noted that it has not been equally successful on the same crop in the Mississippi delta, suggesting that integrated pest management must be carefully adapted to local circumstances.

These examples show that many new (and some

Figure 7.7 TALL WHEATGRASS, a perennial plant, protects winter wheat in an experiment carried out by the U.S. Department of Agriculture Agricultural Research Service near Sidney, Mont. In winter (*upper photograph*) wheatgrass barriers capture snow, forming a uniform layer. Snow insulates dormant plants from the effects of extremely low temperatures. In spring the snow melts, providing the moisture that is needed by wheat plants for early growth. Later the wheat breaks dormancy and begins to grow (*lower phhotograph*), and at that time the wheatgrass serves as a wind barrier.

old) agricultural methods are now finding their way into widespread use. To offset increasing scarcities of land, water and environmental resources, a steady supply of comparable improvements will be needed in the future. If the agricultural-research establishment gets the support it needs (and the record is moderately encouraging), such improvements will in all probability be forthcoming. The much more difficult task, in our judgment, is to create the policies and institutions that will induce farmers to adopt the new technologies and management practices.

Why should that be a problem? After all, conserving scarce resources is good for everyone. Why shouldn't farmers be eager to adopt practices leading to that desirable end? The answer is that the social scarcity of resources is not always communicated faithfully to the level of the individual farm. The underlying reason for that failure is the lack of adequate mechanisms for conveying the signals of scarcity.

A free market, for example, is a mechanism for communicating information about scarcity: the price of a commodity rises as the commodity becomes scarcer. In a market system a resource that is expensive because it is scarce will be treated with the proper regard by the farmer-businessman.

Markets do not function effectively, however, unless clear property rights can be established in the resources that are to be exchanged. This is easier to do for land than for water or for genetic resources, partly because parcels of land can be readily identified and stay in place. As a result, land markets operate in many regions of the world. When land is sold in those regions, landowners reap the benefits of good land management in higher prices or pay the penalty of bad management in lower prices. In this way markets signal conditions of land scarcity and give farmers the incentive to adopt land-conserving technologies.

Markets in water and in genetic diversity are much more difficult to establish. Water is a fugitive resource that moves across hundreds or thousands of miles. As it moves, the same water can be used repeatedly by different individuals or institutions, none of them having exclusive rights to it. Since the essence of a property right is exclusive use, markets for water are poorly developed. Most of the world's irrigation water, both in the developed and in the developing world, is distributed by publicly administered systems. Because these systems are subsidized, the price farmers pay for water (when they pay at all) is usually much less than the value of the water measured according to its social scarcity.

This is a signaling failure. One of its consequences is that farmers have little incentive to adopt water-saving technologies, because they often cost more to install than the (artificially low) amount the farmer saves. That situation is changing in some regions. In the western U.S., water markets have been set up in which various parties, including farmers and municipalities, bid for water rights. In areas where such markets operate, the price of water has generally gone up, indicating that the system is conveying more accurate information about water's scarcity.

There is, however, another side of the question. Water subsidies are deeply rooted in social and political traditions of long standing. Their removal would encounter fierce resistance. It will be of little benefit if policies aimed at saving water evoke social turmoil. The challenge to policymakers is to design policies that carry the needed signal without provoking unacceptably high levels of conflict.

If the concept of a market in water is problematic, that of one in genetic diversity is even less plausible. Who owns diversity? How can it be bought and sold? Yet even here alternatives are available that might imitate the signal-carrying function of markets. There are millions of people around the world who put a high value on the tropical rain forest, which is the basis of much genetic diversity. Such people could form coalitions to pay owners of tropical forests for protecting them. There are formidable obstacles to this idea, but some realization of it has already been seen in the proposal to swap developing-country debt for agreements to protect the rain forest.

The examples of water and genetic diversity suggest it is possible to foster marketlike mechanisms even in areas where that approach would seem intrinsically implausible. But markets do have limits. The difficulty of establishing property rights in environmental resources has encouraged the regulatory approach, in which governmental authorities set limits on particular threats to the environment. The clearest instance in agriculture is the regulation of pesticide production and use, which forces manufacturers and farmers to give more weight to the social scarcity of a pesticide-free environment than they would without regulations.

If marketlike mechanisms rooted in economics cannot be created, then regulations become a necessary tool of social policy. Regulations carry a heavy social cost, however, because they require people to act against their own economic self-interest. This is true by definition; no regulations are needed to get people to act in the direction of economic self-interest. As a result, regulations foster political conflict and must be enforced by some form of bureaucratic apparatus. If the two interests that are on a collision course (society's interest in protecting the environment and the self-interest of the individual farmer) are large, as they are in the case of pesticide use, the social costs of a regulatory approach can be high.

It is our view that in the long run the most successful approaches will rest on merging individual and societal interests rather than on enforcing the one over the other. This is essentially an institutional, not a technological, problem. What is lacking are forms of communication that connect the overarching interest of society in a sustainable agricultural system with the well-being of the individual farmer. Specifically, institutional mechanisms must be devised that correctly signal the emerging social scarcities of land, water and genetic diversity. Finding these mechanisms is the most important policy challenge for the world's agricultural development.

Strategies for Energy Use

Energy efficiency can reconcile environmental concerns with economic development for all nations. It can stretch energy supplies, slow climatic changes and buy time to develop alternative energy resources.

. . .

John H. Gibbons, Peter D. Blair and Holly L. Gwin

Energy fosters human activity. It cooks our food, fuels our transportation system, heats and cools our buildings and powers our industries. Energy helps to sustain a way of life that includes good health, rewarding employment and leisure time. The standard of living enjoyed by the U.S., Japan, West Germany and other industrialized nations results in large part from energy access: one fifth of the world's population consumes more than 70 percent of the world's commercial energy. Yet the industrialized world's energy intensity—the amount of energy used to produce a unit of gross national product—fell by one fifth between 1973 and 1985. In the U.S. the gross national product grew 40 percent while energy consumption remained constant (see Figure 8.2).

The most rapid growth in energy consumption now occurs in developing countries. As they seek to industrialize, raise standards of living and accommodate population growth, the less developed countries, such as China, Mexico and India, must expend more energy. Between 1980 and 1985, population in less developed countries grew by 11 percent and energy consumption grew by 22 percent; corresponding numbers for the industrialized world were 3 and 5 percent. Even so, less developed countries still consume four to seven times less energy per person than do the industrialized countries.

Worldwide energy demand increases even as knowledge of how energy use threatens the global environment grows. Coal and oil combustion produces acid rain, which damages lakes, forests, structures and crops in Europe and North America. Nuclear fission produces long-lived radioactive wastes. Automobiles fill the air with smog, which threatens health and property throughout the industrialized world. Energy consumption dumps more than five billion tons of carbon into the atmosphere each year. The resulting accumulation of carbon dioxide, coupled with other greenhouse gases, could warm the globe several degrees by the middle of the next century, altering the earth's climate at a rate from 10

Figure 8.1 **ENERGY-EFFICIENT BUILDINGS, such as this bank in St. Cloud, Minn., and efficiency technologies for transportation and industry can help provide energy services—shelter, mobility and goods—at lower environmental costs. The building's insulating windows saved the bank $59,000 in heating equipment. A low-emissivity coating blocks heat flow through the windows.**

to 100 times faster than the rate of climatic change at the end of the last ice age.

We seem to be playing out an ancient myth. Prometheus stole fire and wound up chained to a rock, lashed by the seas and burned by the sun. We have captured the power of fossil fuels, and our penalty is the loss of personal and environmental health.

We can change the story. Technological ingenuity can dramatically reduce the amount of energy required to provide a given level of goods and services, simultaneously cutting down on energy-driven problems. Investments in energy efficiency can help us reduce fossil-fuel demand without sacrificing economic growth. Application of existing efficiency technologies can save investment capital, buy time for the development of new supply tech-

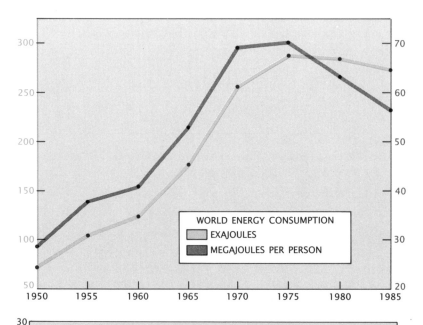

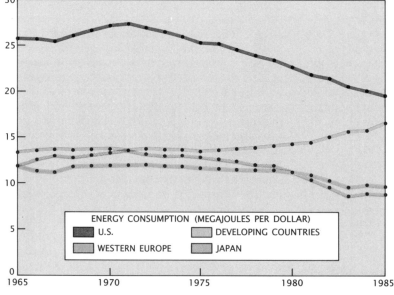

Figure 8.2 WORLD ENERGY CONSUMPTION (*top*) is shown from 1950 to 1985 (*blue*). The red line traces world energy consumption per capita. Energy intensity—consumption divided by gross national product—is shown by region in 1985 dollars (*bottom*). In less developed countries the rise in intensity can be attributed to growth in population and economic activity. Although the U.S. has reduced its intensity by growing economically without consuming more energy, it lags far behind Europe and Japan.

nologies and ultimately make it possible to provide a higher level of goods and services at a given level of energy consumption. In the following discussion we consider the possibilities for new energy resources and increased efficiency. We emphasize efficiency as our best hope.

Humankind expends in one year an amount of fossil fuel that it took nature roughly a million years to produce. Global energy consumption rose from 21 exajoules in 1900 to 318 exajoules in 1988. (An exajoule is 10^{18} joules, approximately one quadrillion British thermal units, or the heat that would be released by burning 170 million barrels of crude oil.) Coal, oil and natural gas supply 88 percent of global energy, and nuclear energy provides most of the rest (see Figure 8.3). Many less developed countries still depend heavily on noncommercial fuels, such as wood, dung and crop wastes, but as their economies develop, they rely increasingly on fossil fuels for commerce and industry.

Oil dominates energy markets, accounting for 38 percent of commercial energy consumption. The Organization of Petroleum Exporting Countries (OPEC) controls three quarters of proved crude-oil reserves, including all recent additions. Reserve estimates have been revised downward for non-OPEC nations, including the Soviet Union, which consumes 15 percent of world oil and has been increasing its production rates.

Dependence on Middle East oil strains the economies of both the less developed and the industrialized world. Expenditures for oil imports have hampered the developing world's efforts to gain hard currency and repay debts. In 1987 the U.S. imported $40 billion worth of oil, an amount equal to one third of the country's trade deficit. During the same year, the Pentagon spent $15 billion to protect oil supplies. As the Soviet Union, the U.S. and other non-OPEC nations deplete their oil reserves, the geopolitics of energy will once again focus on the Middle East.

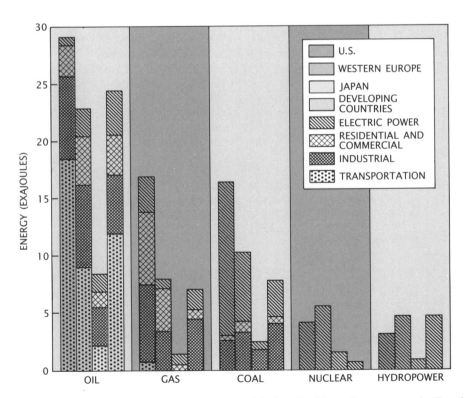

Figure 8.3 ENERGY HABITS differ among nations, but fossil fuels still feed most energy production. The U.S. transportation system alone consumes enough oil to provide for all of Japan's energy needs. Developing nations devote most of their energy to industry.

Natural gas provides a fifth of all commercial energy. It is clean-burning, efficient and flexible enough for use in industry, transportation and power generation. It generates fewer pollutants than any other fossil fuel and less carbon dioxide as well: natural gas releases 14 kilograms of carbon dioxide for every billion joules, whereas oil and coal release 20 and 24 kilograms, respectively. Many industry experts expect conventional sources of natural gas to last four or more decades, and many electric utilities consider natural gas to be the best near-term substitute for oil as a fuel for some power plants. Yet known conventional gas supplies, too, are controlled by only a few nations. The Middle East and the Soviet Union hold nearly 70 percent of these reserves. As conventional supplies dwindle and costs rise, however, large and widely distributed sources of "unconventional" gas such as coal-seam gas may become economical.

World coal reserves total about 950 billion metric tons, and roughly half of them are of high quality. Reserves could last more than 275 years at today's production rates. The U.S. and the Soviet Union each control a quarter of global coal reserves; the rest are spread across Africa, Australia, Europe and Asia (mostly in China). Industrialized countries generate between 20 and 30 percent of their energy from coal. China gets almost three quarters of its total energy from coal.

Coal is a dirty fuel: mining it can ravage the land, and burning it can generate large amounts of carbon dioxide and other pollutants. Environmental concerns could limit coal consumption worldwide, unless technologies to burn it more efficiently or convert it to alternative fuels are adopted. Devices known as precipitators and scrubbers, which can filter out some pollutants, may not be adequate to their task. In the past decade engineers have developed a number of "clean coal" technologies, such as an electric generator that first transforms the coal into natural gas and then burns the gas to drive a turbine. These technologies offer great promise for reducing most pollutants, but they would not reduce coal's carbon dioxide emissions*. Continued heavy reliance on coal may require technologies that can trap carbon dioxide, which will compromise efficiency.

E nvironmental, geopolitical and economic pressures on fossil-fuel use prompt a search for energy alternatives. Many energy planners favor increased reliance on nuclear power, which today generates about 17 percent of the world's electricity, since its use does not emit carbon dioxide or the pollutants that cause acid rain. Light-water reactors (the dominant design), however, are increasingly expensive to build and operate. France obtains about 70 percent of its electricity from nuclear power, but the accidents at Three Mile Island and Chernobyl have tarnished public perception of reactor safety and reliability. Much of the public doubts that adequate radioactive-management techniques exist or can be developed or that a remedy for proliferation of weapons-grade nuclear materials has been found. As a consequence of these handicaps and the growing attractiveness of other energy sources, U.S. utilities have not ordered a new nuclear plant since 1978.

Advanced reactor designs could help restore the promise of nuclear energy. "Passively stable" reactors could be built that would prevent runaway chain reactions without relying on an external control system. Standardized designs could reduce construction costs, licensing complexities and downtime. Perhaps most important, successful demonstration of radioactive waste-disposal capabilities will be critical to widespread public acceptance of nuclear power.

The potential of wresting energy from the fusion of light nuclei is a fond hope for future generations. Fusion, graced with limitless fuel supplies (deuterium) and less troublesome radioactive by-products, avoids many of the frustrations and limitations of nuclear fission. Still, demonstration and commercialization of fusion power will require billions of dollars and is likely to take decades. The scale of the required effort indicates a need not only for government funding but also for international collaboration. Yet few technologies promise more attractive returns on investment.

Solar-energy markets continue to expand, and unlike nuclear power, the price of solar energy continues to drop. Electricity produced by photovoltaic cells, which directly convert sunlight to electricity, now costs 30 cents per kilowatt-hour and is already a common power source for calculators, watches and satellites (see Figure 8.4). These small-scale applications help to sustain the industry as the technology develops, but photovoltaic cells remain more expensive than conventional electricity generation for most applications. Further advances in microelectronics and semiconductors promise to increase efficiency and further reduce costs.

Solar-power generation is taking place on a larger

scale at plants that convert solar energy to heat. In these solar-central-thermal systems, mirrors or lenses focus sunlight onto a receiver containing a fluid that then conducts heat to a conventional electric generator. In February, a company in California opened a solar-thermal plant that is expected to produce power for less than eight cents per kilowatt-hour. (At today's fossil-fuel prices, combustion turbines generate electricity for about three cents per kilowatt-hour.) Research on advanced, lightweight mirrors and better heat-transfer fluids, such as molten salts, may improve these results.

Solar technologies are not sufficiently advanced to supply base electric loads but could boost energy supplies during periods of peak daytime energy consumption in areas like the American Southwest, where sunshine is plentiful and dependable. Solar plants can also be used as part of a pumped storage system, wherein solar-powered pumps raise water to reservoirs, which later feed hydroelectric genera-

tors. Solar power is a natural partner for other types of energy storage as well, such as compressed air, batteries or (conceivably) current-storing superconducting coils.

Hydroelectric power, a mature technology, carries high capital and environmental costs: new dams often result in the destruction of farmlands and the dislocation of population. Although sites are limited in the industrialized world, small-scale hydroelectric power may prove to be a valuable energy source in developing nations.

Biomass, which consists of wood and organic waste, provides energy for much of the world. Conversion of biomass to more useful products, such as methane or alcohol transportation fuels, will increase the value of this energy source. Power plants fueled by urban solid waste may become a modest but economical energy source as garbage-disposal problems worsen, but methods to separate combustible from noncombustible materials and devices to

Figure 8.4 SIGN OF THE TIMES on a mountain highway has lights powered by photovoltaic cells. The price of the cells has dropped rapidly, thereby expanding their market.

Time can be gained to research and develop such innovative technologies, which increase energy supplies, by consuming existing energy resources more efficiently.

control emissions must be perfected. The carbon dioxide emissions associated with burning biomass can be offset by regrowing the plants or trees, thereby renewing the "carbon sink" they initially provided.

Some energy planners view wind power as a promising source of energy. Sweden is considering the replacement of its nuclear reactors with wind turbines anchored to the sea floor. Before wind power can be viewed as a dependable energy source, however, a system must be designed to operate reliably at variable rotor speeds.

Geothermal production of energy, which extracts heat from underground masses of hot rock, and ocean-thermal energy conversion, which exploits the temperature difference between the ocean's warm surface waters and its cold depths, can also contribute substantial amounts of energy in certain regions. For example, more than 2,000 megawatts of geothermal power has been tapped in northern California. In the next several decades, low-temperature applications (for example, for heating greenhouses) could develop into significant markets in some areas.

The conjuncture of the Arab oil embargo and a U.S. coal miners' strike in 1973 heightened concern about the immediate shortage of energy supplies and their ultimate depletion. Analysts of the time fairly consistently projected two things. First, the high rate of growth in energy demand would continue, since a nation's energy consumption was inextricably linked to its economic development. Second, a continuing rise in energy consumption would have disastrous consequences.

Neither projection has been realized so far, in part because higher energy prices expanded the amount of existing supplies but largely because of the massive, unanticipated contributions of energy-efficiency technologies. The most promising opportunities for both industrialized and less developed countries to sustain economic development without the many costs of increased fossil-fuel use lie on the demand side of the energy equation. Improvements in energy efficiency can be implemented much more economically than new supplies of energy can be developed.

The buildings sector of the global economy holds many opportunities for improved energy efficiency (see Figure 8.1). In 1985 buildings in industrialized countries consumed 37 exajoules, almost equal to OPEC's production. New condensing furnaces could significantly reduce this demand. Because they reabsorb much heat from exhaust gases, condensing furnaces need 28 percent less fuel and emit fewer pollutants into the atmosphere than do conventional gas furnaces. Systems for controlling the indoor environment can monitor outdoor and indoor temperatures, sunlight and the location of people and then provide light and conditioned air where needed. These systems typically can provide energy savings of from 10 to 20 percent. A combination of improved lamps, reflectors and daytime lighting can cut the consumption of energy for lighting by 75 percent or more.

Advanced building materials can sharply reduce loss of heat through windows, doors and walls. In "superinsulated" homes, where normal insulation is doubled and a liner forms an airtight seal in walls, heat radiating from people, light, stoves and other appliances alone can warm the house. In comparison with the average home built in the U.S., some superinsulated homes in Minnesota require 68 percent less heat; for some residences in Sweden, the saving is 89 percent.

In industry, sensors and controls, advanced heat-recovery systems and friction-reducing technologies can decrease energy consumption. A great opportunity for improving efficiency is cogeneration—the combined production of heat and electricity. Only a third of the energy from the steam produced by a boiler in a conventional electric-power plant is converted to electricity; in a cogeneration plant, much of the energy remaining in the used steam serves as a heat source for other industrial processes.

Other efficiency measures are specific to each industry. In the paper industry, automated process control, greater process speeds and high-pressure rollers can boost efficiencies significantly. Advanced processes in the steel industry offer energy savings of at least 40 percent in U.S. plants. In developing nations, efficiencies could be improved still further: China and India use four times as much energy to make a ton of steel as Japan does.

New electric-generation technologies promise greater efficiency around the globe. Fluidized-bed combustion, in which burning coal is suspended (fluidized) in a stream of air, can increase efficiency and reduce emission of pollutants. Some analysts feel that the most promising future option for electric-power generation is the aeroderivative turbine, which is based on jet engine designs and burns natural gas. With additional refinement, this technology could raise conversion efficiency from its present value, 33 percent, to more than 45 percent.

Transportation in industrialized and less developed countries constitutes the largest and most rapidly growing drain on the world's oil reserves and is a major threat to the environment. Cars and light trucks consume more than one out of every three barrels of oil and contribute 15 percent of carbon dioxide emissions in the U.S. During the past 15 years, new cars and trucks have become markedly more efficient through strategies such as increased use of light materials, the installation of radial tires to reduce rolling resistance and the redesign of exteriors to decrease aerodynamic drag. Further gains in vehicle efficiency could come from a variety of technologies such as continuously variable transmissions and direct-injection diesel engines.

The technical potential exists to push automobile fuel economy over 65 miles per gallon. If the price of gasoline were to increase in the U.S. to reflect its full costs—economic, environmental and geopolitical—as it has in other nations, U.S. consumers might demand more fuel-efficient cars, and regulations for increased efficiency would make more sense. Even now, U.S. new-car fuel economy could be increased to 33 miles per gallon with existing technology at little cost to consumers. Yet manufacturers resist these steps, fearing consumer backlash, since in many instances lower fuel efficiency can be traded for improved performance. Alternatively, the fuel economy of new cars could be increased from its current level of about 22 miles per gallon to 38 by improving technologies at a cost equal to the value of the gasoline saved over a car's lifetime (calculated at the current average price per gallon of $1.10).

Transportation, communication, manufacturing—all those things we associate with economic development and higher standards of living require energy services. Many technologies exist, however, to supply both necessities and amenities with far less fuel than we currently use. Planning for future energy needs and deciding how much to invest in new supplies or in technologies for efficient use requires a sense of what we can or would like to achieve (see Figure 8.5). Decreasing oil consumption in the U.S., for instance, could significantly protect its economy and increase geopolitical and planetary stability.

Yet even dramatic improvements in energy efficiency will not be sufficient to protect the environment if they are confined to the industrialized world. Economic projections show that if nothing is done to hasten energy-technology development and to move existing efficiency technologies into the market in developing countries, global climatic change and other major environmental problems will escalate beyond acceptable bounds. Even if industrialized countries managed to halve their carbon dioxide emissions (currently 1,800 kilograms per person per year), population growth and economic development in the less developed countries would most likely drive up their carbon dioxide emissions from 450 to 900 kilograms per person per year by 2030. Annual worldwide emissions of carbon dioxide would then be 2.5 times what they are today.

The industrialized world uses the lion's share of

OPPORTUNITIES FOR EFFICIENCY	CAR MILES PER GALLON	HOME THOUSAND JOULES PER SQUARE METER	REFRIGERATOR KILOWATT-HOURS PER DAY	GAS FURNACE MILLION JOULES PER DAY	AIR CONDITIONER KILOWATT-HOURS PER DAY
MODEL AVERAGE	18	190	4	210	10
NEW MODEL AVERAGE	27	110	3	180	7
BEST MODEL	50	68	2	140	5
BEST PROTOTYPE	77	11	1	110	3

Figure 8.5 PLANNING FOR FUTURE ENERGY NEEDS depends on the development of new technologies. Opportunities for greater energy efficiency now exist in housing, transportation, heating and cooling.

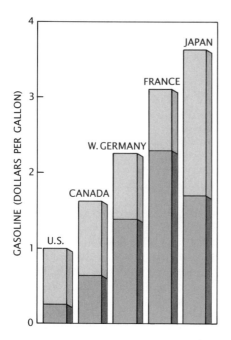

Figure 8.6 GASOLINE PRICES in the U.S. do not reflect the full costs of protecting oil supplies and cleaning the environment. Other nations impose heavy taxes (*red*) on gasoline that force consumers to consider the full impact of their energy habits.

commercial energy, but it has the tools at hand to increase efficiency and decrease fossil-fuel use. One place to start is application of the market rule — "energy prices matter" — to the U.S. transportation system.

The cost of a gallon of gas in the U.S. has reached its lowest level ever. It does not reflect the cost of defense for the Middle East, smog, global warming or the trade imbalance caused by oil imports. Gasoline prices in Europe and Japan are double or triple the U.S. price because governments there impose levies that force consumers to consider and internalize the full costs of their behavior (see Figure 8.6). If Americans want to hold down oil consumption and attendant carbon dioxide emissions and play a world leadership role, a revision of transportation policy to reflect all energy-related costs would be a good place to start.

Policies designed to speed the market penetration of new technologies are also essential. For example, research done at the Lawrence Berkeley Center for Building Science in California indicates that an $8-

million investment in manufacturing and installing low-emissivity windows could eliminate the need for 36 million barrels of oil, which would cost $300 million to produce. Governments may want to take steps to create a preference for investment in efficiency technologies over production. The U.S. Congress did recently pass legislation imposing minimum efficiency standards on all new appliances. This measure was necessary because builders, who seek to minimize initial costs, were eschewing cost-effective technologies to the detriment of building occupants, who are more interested in life-cycle costs.

Efficient lighting, another big energy saver, may also require policy intervention to succeed because of the inherent imperfections of the marketplace. In one promising approach, utilities subsidize customers to replace existing lighting with more efficient equipment; both parties share the savings. Ironically, the same utilities that gave away light bulbs in the 1950's to build electricity demand may now find it in their interest to give away high-efficiency light bulbs to decrease demand in the 1990's.

The developing world's share of energy consumption is small but inefficient, and demand is rapidly growing. With the help of the industrialized world, however, developing countries could apply technical solutions that would promote economic growth while keeping energy-demand growth relatively low. One important analysis shows that application of the best energy technology available today could provide a developing nation with a mid-1970's European level of energy services while increasing energy consumption by only 20 percent over the average consumption of a developing country in 1980. This model also confirms that industrialized countries could continue economic growth but consume less energy than they do today.

Why should less developed countries worry at all about saving energy when their prime concern is generating economic growth, which includes increasing the availability of energy services? The answer is that energy efficiency reconciles the simultaneous goals of development and environmental protection. Efficiency saves capital and decreases the production of carbon dioxide, sulfates (which cause acid rain), hydrocarbons and nuclear waste (see Figure 8.7).

The less developed countries face some hard choices. The path of industrial development in

China, for instance, could have a greater effect on the atmospheric accumulation of carbon dioxide than that of any other nation. China's critical role stems from its large and growing population, its tendency toward energy-intensive processes, its poor energy efficiency and its massive reliance on coal. Between 1980 and 1986 China's manufacturing sector grew by 12 percent a year, the fastest growth in any large nation in the world. The average energy intensity of China's industrial sector has dropped, but it remains higher than the intensity of any other developing nation. Indeed, the potential for improved efficiency is China's chief future energy resource.

Achieving that potential will require large transfers of technology and capital from the industrialized world, but it will also require reform of China's energy-pricing policy. Coal in China is priced at one quarter the international level. Folk wisdom has it that "one ton of coal could not even buy a ton of sand; one barrel of oil could not even buy a bottle of liquor."

Industrialized countries with aging infrastructure will also have a major impact on future energy consumption and carbon emissions. Energy intensity in the Soviet Union is twice the average of nations belonging to the Organization for Economic Cooperation and Development and shows no sign of improvement. The new policies of *perestroika* and *glasnost*, which encourage efficiency, market-oriented systems and global cooperation, therefore hold great promise for the global economy and en-

Figure 8.7 GENERATION OF ELECTRICITY at plants fueled by oil, coal or gas, like this coal-burning plant in San Juan, N.M., accounts for 23 percent of carbon dioxide emissions from energy production as well as for pollutants that cause acid rain. Although emission-control devices can remove the pollutants, an effective method has not yet been devised to capture carbon dioxide.

vironment. As the U.S.S.R., China and other centrally planned economies move toward a more rational price system, they will soon recognize, however, that market prices still do not reflect major external costs. Because we now realize that these costs may include extraordinary global environmental problems, it may be up to more industrialized countries to encourage—through technology transfer, subsidies or loans—policies or technologies that take developing countries beyond the levels of efficiency justifiable on the basis of free-market prices. Such policies would require unprecedented levels of international cooperation.

Capital and ingenuity can substitute for energy throughout the world, but it will take technical sophistication, political will, enlightened economic thinking and time. Much of the technical sophistication needed to guarantee significant increases in the efficiency of energy conversion and use already exists, and efficiency is often cheap compared with the real costs of fossil fuels and the capital costs of new supplies. But research and development, funded both privately and by the government, is necessary to push beyond existing limits. We also need to continue investigating new supplies, especially nuclear energy and renewable energy sources,

so that they can complement and ultimately replace fossil fuels. In the meantime, efficiency improvements will hold down fossil-fuel demand, lessen environmental problems, save investment capital and ultimately enable a given level of amenities to be provided for less energy.

Political will is another matter, as is enlightened economic thinking. Who wants to raise the apparent cost of fuel to the poor, in the U.S. or in India? We may know, rationally, that subsidizing fuel costs imposes far greater burdens on a nation than encouraging and perhaps subsidizing purchases of efficient cars or home appliances, but policy adjustments to foster efficiency will require that we plow through some new emotional territory. Political will is also crucial for exploiting some alternative-energy technologies. Most scientists believe that safe and reliable nuclear waste-disposal technologies are at hand, but the not-in-my-backyard sentiment prevails among the wider populace. What combination of technical, educational and political skills will enable us to reach accord on this issue, which will be critical to any future deployment of nuclear power?

The fact that one country acting alone cannot "cure" global problems compounds the political burden. Yet the sheer magnitude of U.S. energy consumption (see Figure 8.8) indicates that the U.S. could have a significant impact on global carbon

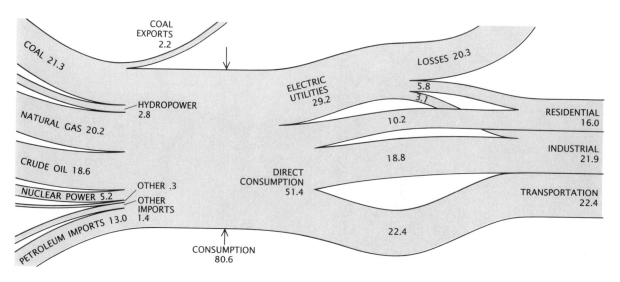

Figure 8.8 ENERGY FLOW shows that in 1987 the U.S. consumed 12.2 exajoules more than it produced. The balance was maintained largely through petroleum imports. Alternative energy resources accounted for only 12 percent of total energy production.

emissions by instituting savings within the cost-effective ranges established by existing technology. And the U.S., because of its energy-intensive past and present and its great technological ingenuity and capability, can be charged with great responsibility in effecting the transition to an era beyond fossil fuels. To do so, it must increase its own efficiency, develop a new array of energy sources and expand the energy possibilities for other countries. The U.S. might consider a twofold goal: first, increase the fraction of useful energy produced from nonfossil resources (by fuel substitution and more efficient combustion) by 20 percent by the end of this century; second, increase the output of goods and services provided per unit of energy consumed by at least 2.5 percent a year for at least two decades. Such goals are challenging but achievable and

could be a useful focus for the U.S. to assume leadership on this truly global issue.

But it is the collective response of developing countries to opportunities for efficient resource use in their economies that will determine humanity's ultimate success in slowing the deterioration of the global environment. New technology can help less developed countries to leap over the undesirable practices of the past and follow new energy paths for development. The industrialized world and developing countries must work together to ensure that opportunities are available and, when sensible, are accepted. Investment in energy-efficiency technologies, which often cost the same as the fuels they displace, represents the most sensible energy path available today. The challenges are great, but so are the opportunities.

Strategies for Manufacturing

Wastes from one industrial process can serve as the raw materials for another, thereby reducing the impact of industry on the environment.

. . .

Robert A. Frosch and Nicholas E. Gallopoulos

People create new technologies and industries to meet human needs more effectively and at lower cost. Innovation is a major agent of progress, and yet innovators' incomplete knowledge sometimes leads to undesirable side effects. Such unforeseen consequences of new inventions are not unique to the feverish industrialization of the 19th and 20th centuries. The ancient Greek myths tell of Pandora and the box full of plagues, of Prometheus punished for stealing fire from the gods and of Icarus, who plummeted from the sky when the sun's heat melted the wax of his wings. In historical times the shift from rawhide to tanned leather, although it made for garments and tools that lasted much longer and were more comfortable to wear and use, brought stenches and disease, so that tan-

Figure 9.1 INDUSTRIAL PLANTS such as this oil refinery in New Jersey make the products and materials that sustain modern life. They also emit pollutants that are difficult to dispose of and that may have long-lasting adverse effects on the environment. Meeting environmental needs calls for manufacturing plants that not only produce goods more efficiently but also fit together into a more harmonious industrial ecosystem. At the same time, consumers must learn to use those products less wastefully.

neries had to be segregated from the communities they served.

Today such inadvertent effects can have a global impact. Consider, for example, the invention of chlorinated fluorocarbons. Before CFC's were developed in the 1930's, refrigerator compressors contained ammonia or sulfur dioxide; either chemical was toxic, and leaks killed or injured many people. CFC's saved lives, saved money and provided such elements of modern life as air-conditioned buildings and untainted food. Only later did atmospheric scientists determine that CFC's contribute to global warming and affect the chemistry of the upper atmosphere, where they destroy ozone.

Such failures should not diminish the fact that technology has improved the lot of people everywhere. Standards of living in many parts of the world are better today than they were 20 or 30 years ago. Many of the adverse effects of industrialization have been brought under control by further applications of technology. Yet as the world's population and standard of living increase, some of the old solutions to industrial pollution and everyday wastes no longer work. There is often no "other side of town" where the modern equivalents of tanneries can be put, no open space beyond the village gates where garbage can be dumped and do no harm.

By the year 2030, 10 billion people are likely to live on this planet; ideally, all would enjoy standards of living equivalent to those of industrial democracies such as the U.S. or Japan. If they consume critical natural resources such as copper, cobalt, molybdenum, nickel and petroleum at current U.S. rates, and if new resources are not discovered or substitutes developed, such an ideal would last a decade or less (see Figure 9.2). On the waste side of the ledger, at current U.S. rates 10 billion people would generate 400 billion tons of solid waste every year—enough to bury greater Los Angeles 100 meters deep.

These calculations are not meant to be forecasts of a grim future. Instead they emphasize the incentives for recycling, conservation and a switch to alternative materials. They lead to the recognition that the traditional model of industrial activity—in which individual manufacturing processes take in raw materials and generate products to be sold plus waste to be disposed of—should be transformed into a more integrated model: an industrial ecosystem. In such a system the consumption of energy and materials is optimized, waste generation is minimized and the effluents of one process—whether they are spent catalysts from petroleum refining, fly and bottom ash from electric-power generation or discarded plastic containers from consumer products—serve as the raw material for another process (see Figure 9.3).

The industrial ecosystem would function as an analogue of biological ecosystems. (Plants synthesize nutrients that feed herbivores, which in turn feed a chain of carnivores whose wastes and bodies eventually feed further generations of plants.) An ideal industrial ecosystem may never be attained in practice, but both manufacturers and consumers must change their habits to approach it more closely if the industrialized world is to maintain its standard of living—and the developing nations are to raise theirs to a similar level—without adversely affecting the environment.

If both industrialized and developing nations embrace changes, it will be possible to develop a more closed industrial ecosystem, one that is more sus-

ESTIMATED LIFETIMES OF SOME GLOBAL RESOURCES

	CURRENT CONSUMPTION RATES		2030 RATES	
	RESERVES	RESOURCES	RESERVES	RESOURCES
ALUMINUM	256	805	124	407
COPPER	41	277	4	26
COBALT	109	429	10	40
MOLYBDENUM	67	256	8	33
NICKEL	66	163	7	16
PLATINUM GROUP	225	413	21	39
COAL	206	3226	29	457
PETROLEUM	35	83	3	7

Figure 9.2 WORLD STOCKS of some essential raw materials will drop perilously low if less developed countries increase their consumption to match that of the industrialized world. Figures show reserves (quantities that can be profitably extracted with current technology) and re-sources (total quantities thought to exist). Estimates of years left until depletion are based on current global consumption (*left*) or on the assumption that in 2030 a population of 10 billion will consume at current U.S. rates (*right*).

tainable in the face of decreasing supplies of raw materials and increasing problems of waste and pollution. Industrialized nations will have to make major and minor changes in their current practices. Developing nations will have to leapfrog older, less ecologically sound technologies and adopt new methods more compatible with the ecosystem approach.

Materials in an ideal industrial ecosystem are not depleted any more than those in a biological one are; a chunk of steel could potentially show up one year in a tin can, the next year in an automobile and 10 years later in the skeleton of a building. Manufacturing processes in an industrial ecosystem simply transform circulating stocks of materials from one shape to another; the circulating stock decreases when some material is unavoidably lost, and it increases to meet the needs of a growing population. Such recycling still requires the expenditure of energy and the unavoidable generation of wastes and harmful by-products, but at much lower levels than are typical today.

Today's industrial operations do not form an ideal industrial ecosystem, and many subsystems and processes are less than perfect. Yet there are developments that could be cause for optimism. Some manufacturers are already making use of "designed offal," or "engineered scrap," in the manufacture of metals and some plastics: tailoring the production of waste from a manufacturing process so that the waste can be fed directly back into that process or into a related one. Other manufacturers are designing packaging to incorporate recycled materials wherever possible or are finding innovative uses for materials that were formerly considered wastes.

Three examples delineate some of the issues involved in developing self-sustaining industrial process systems: the conversion of petroleum derivatives to plastics, the conversion of iron ore to steel, and the refining and use of platinum-group metals as catalysts. We have picked these examples because each represents a different stage in the evolution of a closed cycle. Examining their workings and shortcomings should provide insight into how subsystems can be improved so as to develop an industrial ecosystem.

The iron cycle, in which recycling is well established, is a very mature process with a history dating back thousands of years, even though extensive production of steel did not begin until the 19th century. The plastics cycle, in which reuse is just beginning to make its mark, is less than 100 years old; the first completely synthetic plastic, Bakelite, was introduced shortly after the turn of the century. The platinum-group-metals cycle—in which reuse is common because of the high cost of the materials involved—is even younger: industrial noble-metal catalysts became widely used only in the early 1950's, and the widespread use of noble metals to reduce pollution from automotive exhaust dates back less than 15 years.

The plastics system is potentially highly efficient, but realizing that potential poses challenges that have yet to be met. Plastics are a diverse group of chemically complex compounds whose use has grown explosively, so that they now present a growing disposal problem. Plastics are formed into any number of products, and different plastic resins are difficult to distinguish. This difficulty leads to problems in collection, separation and recycling. Moreover, breaking plastics down to their original chemical constituents is often technologically infeasible or economically unattractive.

The drawbacks of plastics must nonetheless be weighed against their benefits. Plastic containers, for example, are safer than the glass containers they replace. Countless injuries, from minor cuts to severe lacerations, have been prevented by the substitution of plastic for glass in milk bottles and containers for bathroom products such as shampoo. Plastic containers are generally lighter than glass or metal ones, so that less energy is required to transport them; they also require less energy to make than glass or metal containers, especially if they are recycled. The Midwest Research Institute in Kansas City, Mo., determined that compared with glass containers, half-gallon polyvinyl chloride (PVC) containers require less than half the energy to produce and transport and consume one twentieth the mass of raw materials and less than one third as much water in their manufacture. They also generate less than half of the waste of glass manufacturing.

Each kind of plastic poses different problems depending on its particular composition and use. PVC, of which almost four million tons are produced every year in the U.S., is a particularly dramatic example of the complex threats plastics pose to the environment. PVC, which accounts for about one sixth of total plastic production, is made into products ranging from pipes to automobile parts to shampoo bottles. Its production requires both hydrocarbons and chlorine. (The chlorine makes the plastic's impact on the environment greater than it would be if only hydrocarbons were required—as is the case for polyethylene, for example.) Natural gas is the most commonly used feedstock for PVC in the U.S.; elsewhere it is naphtha, a petroleum fraction. In either case the feedstock is converted to ethylene, which is chlorinated to form vinyl chloride monomer; the monomer molecules are then linked to form PVC.

The efficiency of the production process has already been improved. For example, manufacturers have developed more efficient membrane cells for the electrolysis of sodium chloride to produce the required chlorine. (The sodium chloride, common table salt, is dissolved in cells through which a current flows; sodium ions migrate to one electrode, and chlorine ions migrate to the other. A membrane separates the two electrodes.) The membrane cells also eliminate the asbestos and mercury required in older electrolysis cells, thus reducing hazardous wastes.

Even so, the PVC production process exemplifies classic "end of pipe" control measures for reducing pollutants. Emissions of vinyl chloride monomer during manufacturing are tightly controlled, a practice instituted when it became known that the monomer is both toxic and carcinogenic. Unreacted vinyl chloride is generally stripped from the finished PVC by low-pressure steam. Most of the monomer is recovered and recycled, but some of it is present at concentrations too low for easy recovery and recycling; instead it is sent to an incinerator to be broken down. Scrubbers remove hydrochloric acid from the exhaust.

Recycling of PVC during manufacturing is fairly straightforward. Plants that make PVC products typically recycle almost all of their in-house scrap. At General Motors, for example, scrap generated in the manufacture of PVC parts such as decorative trim, seat covers and dashboards is segregated by color, reground, melted and used along with virgin PVC.

Once plastic enters the consumer market, however, recycling becomes considerably more complicated. Only about 1 percent of the PVC discarded by consumers is recycled. The wide range of products in which PVC is found makes collection and recovery more difficult, but it also creates interesting opportunities. For example, potential health hazards and liability concerns prevent recycled plastics from being incorporated into containers where the plastic touches food; recycled bottles may find their way into drainage pipes instead.

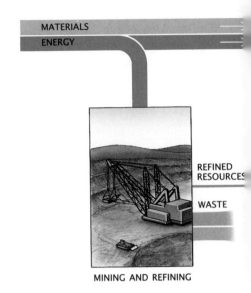

MATERIALS

ENERGY

REFINED RESOURCES

WASTE

MINING AND REFINING

Figure 9.3 INDUSTRIAL-ECOSYSTEM CYCLE starts with resources and progresses to a finished product that can be recycled (*blue*) after use to enter the cycle again as a

Other vinyl products that cannot easily be recycled can be burned to produce heat or electricity. PVC contains roughly as much energy as wood or paper, but its chlorine content poses problems: incinerators that burn PVC must have scrubbers to prevent emissions of hydrochloric acid, which contribute to acid rain. During combustion the chlorine can also form small amounts of dioxins, which are believed to be potent carcinogens. As a result, the incineration of discarded PVC is discouraged. Although recent tests by the New York State Energy Research and Development Authority have shown that properly designed and operated incinerators do not emit significant quantities of hydrochloric acid or dioxins, environmentalists and regulators are not convinced that incinerators would achieve such low emission levels in practice.

Because of its chlorine content, PVC is a worst-case example of the problems plastics pose. Other polymers such as polypropylene and polyethylene present fewer environmental hazards. They have physical properties similar to those of PVC, but they contain no chlorine. Polyethylene terephthalate (PET), the material used in carbonated beverage bottles, is recycled in nine states that have manda-

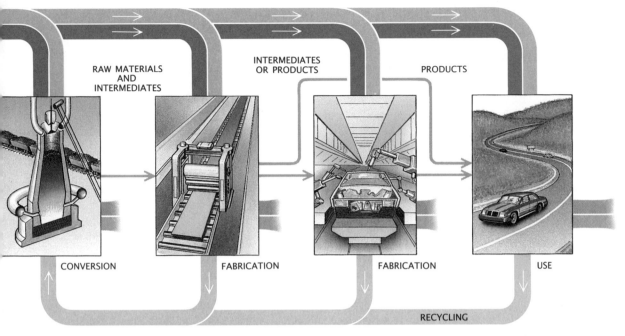

RAW MATERIALS AND INTERMEDIATES

INTERMEDIATES OR PRODUCTS

PRODUCTS

CONVERSION

FABRICATION

FABRICATION

USE

RECYCLING

raw material. (The iron and steel cycle is shown here.) At each stage in the manufacturing process, energy (*red*) and additional raw materials (*green*) are added, and waste heat and by-products are generated. In an optimal cycle, wastes are captured and reused either in the same manufacturing process or in a different one.

tory deposit laws: California, Connecticut, Delaware, Maine, Massachusetts, Michigan, New York, Oregon and Vermont. Bottles collected in these states account for 150 million of the 750 million pounds of PET resin produced every year. Recyclers pay from $100 to $140 per ton of PET, making it the second most valuable component of municipal solid waste after aluminum. The PET is reconstituted into resins for injection molding to produce products ranging from automobile parts to electronic devices or is spun into polyester fibers that go into pillows, stuffed furniture, insulated clothing and carpeting.

As the infrastructure for collecting and sorting PET and other consumer plastics grows, recycling rates should increase significantly. According to recyclers such as Wellman Inc., of Shrewsbury, N.J., which currently processes about 100 million pounds of PET a year (see Figure 9.4), the market for recycled plastics is limited by collection efficiency rather than by demand.

The industrial system for iron presents a different picture. Techniques for recycling are well established, and there is a strong infrastructure for collecting scrap. Yet discarded metal continues to pile up in scrapyards and across the U.S. because there is not enough demand for it. Elemental iron, the predominant component of both steel and cast iron, is the backbone of modern life: it is used in roads, in the automobiles that pass over the roads and in buildings. In the U.S. iron production begins when ore is mined in huge open pits as deep as 100 meters or more. The ore is concentrated and formed into pellets at the mine and then converted into pig iron in a blast furnace, where it is heated with coke, limestone and air. The coke adds carbon to the mix, and the limestone and the oxygen in the air react with impurities in the ore to form slag, which is then removed. Small admixtures of other elements yield steel to be cast, rolled or forged into billets, slabs, beams or sheets.

Once iron has been formed into products, which are eventually discarded, its properties (especially its ferromagnetism) facilitate identification and separation. The enormous amount of iron in circulation makes recycling relatively easy and economically attractive. It is not surprising, therefore, that every year millions of tons of scrap join iron ore to produce steel products. The scrap generated by stamping steel parts for automobiles, for example, is recycled into engine blocks and other castings. All four foundries that GM operates rely entirely on scrap steel obtained from other GM operations and on scrap iron generated during the casting process (see Figure 9.5).

Although iron recycling is a relatively simple process, the system is not a closed loop. Much of the scrap from discarded consumer products is not recovered but is scattered around the countryside, where it corrodes away a little every year and is considered a blight rather than an asset. In 1982 recoverable iron scrap amounted to 610 million tons; at the end of 1987 the figure had risen to more than 750 million. A major reason for the increase is that U.S. production of iron and steel during this period was the lowest it had been since the end of World War II. The demand for scrap to make steel decreased while iron and steel products continued to be scrapped at the previous rate.

Shifting patterns of steel manufacturing, both in the U.S. and around the globe, are responsible for the increase in scrap. One subtle culprit is a technology shift from open-hearth furnaces to basic oxygen furnaces for producing steel. Basic oxygen furnaces (so called because they make steel in a large closed vessel supplied with pressurized oxygen) require only 25 tons of scrap steel to be mixed with every 100 tons of pig iron from the blast furnace, as opposed to a nearly equal mix for the open hearth.

The shift to basic oxygen furnaces began in the U.S. about 1958, and today open-hearth furnaces account for less than 3 percent of total production. Open-hearth furnaces were replaced to improve manufacturing efficiency and reduce air pollution, but their disappearance led to a decline in iron recycling. In making these changes, steelmakers had no economic mechanism for taking account of the adverse environmental impacts of scrap accumulation or the possible long-term effects of consuming more iron ore for each unit of steel.

More recently minimills have been built that rely on electric-arc furnaces and consume scrap steel almost exclusively. These low-volume mills have increased their share of U.S. steel production, but not enough to compensate for the lost demand for scrap to feed open-hearth furnaces. Furthermore, minimills produce only a limited range of steel products, and many of those products must be made from scrap containing very low levels of impurities. Scrap that contains excess copper, for example, is not suitable for making sheet steel, because the resulting sheet is too brittle to form into

products. If electric-arc furnaces are to make significant inroads into the U.S. stock of scrap iron, they must be coupled to production facilities that produce a wider range of products, and better techniques must be developed for dealing with impure scrap.

Platinum-group metals (platinum, palladium, rhodium, ruthenium, iridium and osmium) were, until the mid-1970's, part of a very efficient industrial system. These metals were once recycled with efficiencies of 85 percent or better, but the advent of catalytic converters for automobiles dealt this system a shock from which recycling rates are only now beginning to recover.

Recycling of platinum-group metals is dictated not so much by the environmental effects of their disposal as by their limited supply and the difficulties of mining and refining them. Ores contain only about seven parts per million of mixed platinum-group metals, so that about 20 million metric tons a

Figure 9.4 BEVERAGE CONTAINERS, seen here bound into bales at a major recycling center in New Jersey, can be reprocessed into plastic products such as polyester fiber and molded parts. Some 150 million pounds of bottles made from polyethylene terephthalate (PET) were collected last year from the nine U.S. states that have mandatory deposit laws; 750 million pounds are produced nationwide.

year must be refined to produce 143 tons of purified metals—an amount that could fit into a cube roughly two meters on a side.

About 60 percent of the platinum-group metals mined is formed into metal products such as jewelry, ingots for investors and chemical-reaction vessels; these products are eventually recycled with almost complete efficiency. The remainder is used to make chemicals and catalysts for chemical plants, petroleum refineries and automobiles (see Figure 9.6). Catalysts adsorb molecules on their surfaces and promote chemical reactions that either join the molecules together or break them into smaller ones. Catalytic converters for automobiles, which reduce exhaust emissions of hydrocarbons, carbon monoxide and oxides of nitrogen, are the most rapidly growing use of platinum-group metals; consumption rose from about 11.5 metric tons in 1975 to about 40 in 1988. Automobiles currently account for most of the yearly permanent consumption of platinum-group metals.

Platinum-group metals in industrial applications are recycled quite efficiently. Each plant uses large amounts of catalyst, so that the payoffs from recycling are clear. Used catalysts are generally recycled every few months, providing a large, continuing stream of materials for reclaimers to process. In chemical and pharmaceutical plants, for example, catalysts are typically recycled in less than a year, and about 85 percent of the platinum-group metals in them are recovered. Some petroleum refineries are even more successful, recovering up to 97 percent of their noble metals.

The automotive pattern of noble-metal use stands in sharp contrast to that of the process industries: there are tens of millions of catalytic converters, each of which contains only a few grams of platinum-group metals (less than two grams of platinum, for example), and the lifespan of about 10 years for an average car makes for a much slower turnover of recyclable materials. As a result, only about 12 percent of the platinum-group metals in catalytic converters is currently recycled.

Poor recycling rates for automotive catalysts can

Figure 9.5 SCRAP METAL from the casting and machining of engine parts awaits recycling at a General Motors foundry in Defiance, Ohio. The company operates four foundries; they are supplied entirely by scrap from sheet-metal stamping, iron casting and machining operations. Despite the relative ease with which scrap can be recycled, millions of tons pile up every year in U.S. scrapyards for lack of ready markets.

be blamed almost entirely on the lack of an effective means for collecting discarded converters. The technology for recovering platinum-group metals from the converters is quite well understood; a plant opened by Texasgulf Minerals & Metals, Inc., in Ala. in 1984 recovers 90 percent of the platinum, 90 percent of the palladium and 80 percent of the rhodium from used converters. Millions of individual converters, however, are dispersed among thousands of scrapyards and almost 2,000 automotive scrap recyclers. The cost of locating, collecting and emptying the converters and then transporting the catalyst to a reprocessing plant is sufficiently high so that recycling is not profitable for most refining operations unless the price of platinum exceeds $500 an ounce.

The outlook for catalytic-converter recycling is improving. Now that most of the first-generation of cars built with catalytic converters have found their way to U.S. scrapyards, there is a large, continuing flow of raw materials for recyclers. More important, an infrastructure for collecting spent converters is being established. Even Japanese companies such as Nippon Engelhard have set up collecting organizations in the U.S. to acquire automotive catalysts for reprocessing in Japan. In addition the introduction of more stringent emissions controls in Europe, where catalytic converters have not been required, will increase the demand for platinum-group metals, making recycling more profitable.

The life cycles of plastics, iron and the platinum-group metals illustrate some of the issues involved in creating sustainable industrial systems.

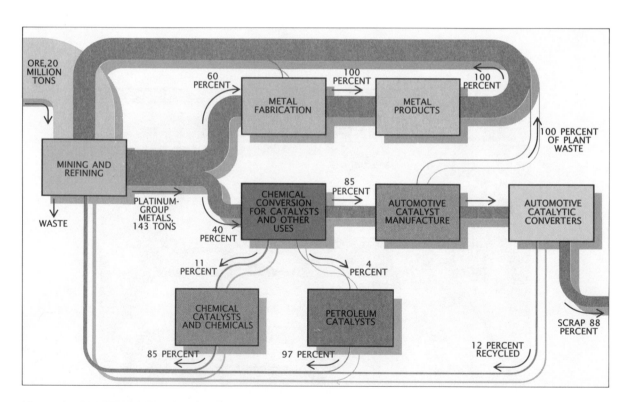

Figure 9.6 PLATINUM-GROUP METALS are recovered efficiently from jewelry and other fabricated objects, two uses that constitute about 60 percent of consumption. Industrial catalysts and chemicals, also efficiently recycled, account for another 6 percent. The fastest-growing use for the metals is in automotive catalytic converters, an application marked by low recycling rates. The infrastructure is only now being set up to collect the millions of converters that enter automotive scrapyards each year and to recover the approximately two grams of platinum (worth about $32 in mid-1989) in each converter.

Equally important is the way in which the inputs and outputs of individual processes are linked within the overall industrial ecosystem. This linkage is crucial for building a closed or nearly closed system.

Like their biological counterparts, individual manufacturing processes in an effective industrial ecosystem contribute to the optimal function of the entire system. Processes are required that minimize the generation of unrecyclable wastes (including waste heat) as well as minimize the permanent consumption of scarce material and energy resources. Individual manufacturing processes cannot be considered in isolation. A process that produces relatively large quantities of waste that can be used in another process may be preferable to one that produces smaller amounts of waste for which there is no use.

A good example of the subtleties involved is the dematerialization of manufactured goods—the use of plastics, composites and high-strength alloys to reduce the mass of products. The trend toward dematerialization has drawn increasing attention in recent years. The mass of a typical automobile, for example, has decreased by more than 400 kilograms since 1975; about 100 kilograms of the decrease are due to the substitution of aluminum and plastics for steel. Lighter cars burn less gasoline. Steel, however, is easy to recycle, whereas the composite plastics that have replaced it resist reuse. The net result may be an immediate drop in fuel consumption but an overall increase in the amount of permanent waste created and in the resources consumed.

Waste-minimization activities in U.S. industries have been aided by regulations developed in the late 1970's to control hazardous-waste disposal. The regulations, reflecting long-term environmental costs, have increased the cost of landfill disposal from less than $20 a ton to $200 a ton or more, making alternatives to disposal profitable. Many companies find it profitable to sell their wastes as raw materials. For example, Meridian National in Ohio, a midwestern steel-processing company, reprocesses the sulfuric acid with which it removes scale from steel sheets and slabs, reuses the acid and sells ferrous sulfate compounds to magnetic-tape manufacturers.

If the production of unrecyclable wastes is to be eliminated, similar steps must be taken for each of the low-level by-products in large streams of process effluents. Although emissions at each stage of such manufacturing processes may be relatively small, taken together they can cause serious pollution problems. Minimizing each of these myriad smaller emissions one at a time is a complex and potentially costly challenge (see Figure 9.1).

The challenge can be met in part by implementing a multitude of relatively small changes. Some chemical plants and oil refineries, for example, have significantly reduced their hazardous-waste output by simply changing their procedures for buying and storing cleaning solutions and other low-volume chemicals. By doing so, they have been able to eliminate the need to dispose of leftover amounts.

At ARCO's Los Angeles refinery complex, a series of relatively low-cost changes have reduced waste volumes from about 12,000 tons a year during the early 1980's to about 3,400 today, generating revenue and saving roughly $2 million a year in disposal costs. The company sells its spent alumina catalysts to Allied Chemical and its spent silica catalysts to cement makers. Previously these materials were classified as hazardous wastes and had to be disposed of in landfills at a cost of perhaps $300 a ton.

Alkaline carbonate sludge from a water-softening operation at the refinery goes to a sulfuric acid manufacturer a few miles away, where it neutralizes acidic wastewater. (The acid manufacturer previously purchased pure sodium hydroxide for the same purpose.) A few outflow pipes have been re-routed to improve access for loading, and plant personnel must track the pH of their sludge, but the total investment has been minimal.

The ARCO refinery has also started to recover oil from internal spills and other wastes in a new $1-million recycling facility. When the recycler is fully operational next year, it is expected to reduce wastes by another 2,000 tons. Off-site treatment or landfilling will still be needed for miscellaneous wastes such as solvents, spray cans and the several hundred tons of asbestos insulation being removed from the plant each year.

ARCO's situation is not unique; other major refiners and chemical manufacturers are engaged in similar efforts. For example, investments of $300,000 in process changes and recovery equipment at Ciba-Geigy's Toms River plant in New Jersey reduced disposal costs by more than $1.8 million between 1985 and 1988. Dow Chemical established a separate unit to recover excess hydrochloric acid, which it then either recycles to acid-using processes or sells on the open market. The operation recovers a million tons of acid a year at a profit of $20 million.

By-products and effluents created during manufacturing represent only the supply side of the industrial ecosystem. The demand side is the consumer, who takes in manufactured goods and produces scrap that could be the raw materials for the next cycle of production. If the industrial-ecosystem approach is to become widespread, changes in manufacturing must be matched by changes in consumers' demand patterns and in the treatment of materials once they have been purchased and used.

The behavior of consumers in the U.S. today constitutes an aberration in both time and space (see Figure 9.7). Whereas a typical New Yorker, for example, discards nearly two kilograms of solid waste every day, a resident of Hamburg or Rome throws out only about half that—as New Yorkers did at the turn of the century. Moreover, U.S. consumer habits and waste-management practices form a complex pattern that hinders efforts to reduce waste generation and the growing pressure on municipal landfills. The vast bulk of consumer wastes consists of organic materials and plastics that could relatively easily be composted, recycled or burned to produce energy but instead are stored in landfills, for which land was readily available in the past and where costs were low.

Today, as landfills across the U.S. near capacity, many communities have initiated garbage-sorting programs to reduce the amount of unrecycled waste; more initiatives are likely to follow. Some other countries have already instituted fairly sophisticated collection and treatment practices that go well beyond standard sorting and recycling. Japan, Sweden and Switzerland, for example, have set up collection centers for batteries from portable radios and other consumer products. The batteries contain heavy metals that render composted wastes unsuitable for fertilizing crops; the metals also contaminate fly and bottom ash from incinerators, so that the ash must be disposed of as hazardous waste.

An effective infrastructure for collecting and segregating various consumer wastes can dramatically improve the efficiency of the industrial ecosystem. The American consumer may have to stop heedlessly generating huge volumes of unsorted wastes, but living standards in the U.S. as a whole will not be affected. Moreover, landfills for municipal wastes are running out of space as rapidly as are those for industrial waste; consumers will soon find themselves facing the same economic incentives for waste reduction that producers face today.

Creating a sustainable industrial ecosystem is highly desirable from an environmental perspective and in some cases is highly profitable as well. Nonetheless, there are a number of barriers to its successful implementation. Corporate and public attitudes must change to favor the ecosystem approach, and government regulations must become more flexible so as not to unduly hinder recycling and other strategies for waste minimization.

Federal hazardous-waste regulations are a case in point. They sometimes make waste minimization more difficult than waste disposal. Because of the strict requirements for handling and documenting the treatment of wastes classified as hazardous, many companies choose to buy their materials through conventional channels rather than involve themselves in the regulatory process. A few states do encourage innovative treatment of wastes: California, for example, publishes a biannual catalogue that attempts to match waste generators with waste buyers—manufacturers who need the materials they produce. About half a million tons of hazardous wastes that would otherwise have gone to landfills were recycled in 1987. A dozen other state, provincial and regional waste exchanges operate throughout the U.S. and Canada.

In addition to promoting innovative waste-minimization schemes, governments need to focus on the economic incentives for sustainable manufacturing. Increased landfill costs have forced companies to improve industrial processes and reduce unrecyclable waste, but many small emissions are still controlled by classic end-of-pipe regulations that specify how much of each pollutant may be discharged. Companies must meet regulatory requirements, but there are no direct advantages for manufacturers who capture and treat low-level effluents or who shift to production processes with more benign by-products.

Conventional economic methods take into account only the immediate effects of production decisions. If a manufacturer produces nonrecyclable containers, for example, taxpayers at large bear the increased landfill costs; if a power plant reduces emissions that cause acid rain, communities elsewhere are likely to reap the benefits. Returns to the manufacturer or utility are generally indirect.

Instead of absolute rules, economists have long advocated financial incentives to reduce pollution. These include investment or research credits, tax relief, or fees or taxes imposed on manufacturers according to the amount and nature of the hazardous materials they produce. Such measures can help pay for treatment or disposal; more important, they give companies an incentive to change their manufacturing processes so as to reduce hazardous-waste production. Fees and taxes for pollution make environmental costs internal, so that they can be taken into account when making production decisions (see Chapter 11, "Toward a Sustainable World," by William D. Ruckelshaus).

Pollution fees have come under fire from environmentalists and industrialists as "licenses to pollute" and as "distortions of the market." Both criticisms are potentially valid. Companies can treat fees that are too low as a cost of doing business and pass them on to customers; fees that are too high may force companies to reduce emissions of specific pollutants without regard to other environmental effects or to financial burdens.

Suitably set charges or incentives, however, can be an effective means for manufacturers to incorporate societal costs of pollution and waste into their cost accounting systems. As in the case of rising landfill fees for hazardous wastes, cost feedback for other pollutants could make it more attractive to solve problems at the source rather than to destroy or dispose of effluents once they have been created. Such fees enable manufacturers to share in the overall economic savings accruing from reduced levels of hazardous materials. Providing economic incentives would harness manufacturers' strong competitive drive to reduce costs. Indeed, manufacturers who ignore this imperative perish from the marketplace, a situation that would not change if the societal costs of pollution were allocated to them.

Economic incentives alone are not enough to make the industrial-ecosystem approach commonplace. Traditional manufacturing processes are designed to maximize the immediate benefits to the manufacturer and the consumer of individual products in the economy rather than to the economy as a whole. A holistic approach will be required if the proper balance between narrowly defined economic benefits and environmental needs is to be achieved. (Broadly defined, of course, economic and environmental goals are the same: bad places to live do not make for good markets.)

Figure 9.7 CONSUMER WASTES strain the capacity of landfills such as this one in Deptford, N.J. The environmental problems posed could be avoided by changes in disposal habits. Sorting trash to facilitate the recycling of paper, glass and plastics could simultaneously slow the filling of landfills and reduce the consumption of scarce resources.

The concepts of industrial ecology and system optimization must be taught more widely. Current engineering and technological education either omit these concepts entirely or teach them in such a limited way that they have little impact on the approaches taken to the environmental problems associated with manufacturing. Changing the content of technological education, however, will not be enough. The concepts of industrial ecology must be recognized and valued by public officials, industry leaders and the media. They must be instilled into the social ethos and adopted by government as well as industry.

Government regulation of emissions at the local, national and international level will continue to play a strong role in the transition from traditional methods of manufacturing to an industrial-ecosystem approach. The transition to an ecosystem approach would be accelerated by the early adoption of economic incentives as part of the regulatory system.

To make regulation as effective as possible, officials must base their policies on sound technology and make allowance for technological change. Rules must be cast so as to encourage (or at least not discourage) the development of alternative processes and innovative methods for dealing with industrial by-products. Regulators must take advantage of industry's technological know-how so as to avoid counterproductive control measures. Such a wise regulatory framework will be almost impossible to construct unless government, industry and environmental groups abandon their current adversarial relationships and work together to solve their shared problems.

Even with an industrial-ecosystem approach in place, decisions about how best to allocate resources will not always be easy. Petroleum, for example, is not just a source of energy but also a raw material essential for manufacturing chemicals, plastics and other materials. Some analysts have argued that it should be used only as a raw material and not for energy. A similar argument could be made for using coal as a feedstock instead of as a fuel. On the output side, plastics can be burned for energy, recycled into new products or even reduced to their chemical constituents; it is not clear which choice is unequivocally sounder. Careful analysis of the consequences by "industrial ecologists" will be required to answer such questions.

The ideal ecosystem, in which the use of energy and materials is optimized, wastes and pollution are minimized and there is an economically viable role for every product of a manufacturing process, will not be attained soon. Current technology is often inadequate to the task, and some of the knowledge needed to define the problems fully is lacking. The difficulties in implementing an industrial ecosystem are daunting, especially given the complexities involved in harmonizing the desires of global industrial development with the needs of environmental safety.

Nonetheless, we are optimistic. The incentive for industry is clear: companies will be able to minimize costs and stay competitive while adhering to a rational economic approach that accounts for global costs and benefits. Equally clear are the benefits to society at large: people will have a chance to raise their visible standards of living without incurring hidden environmental penalties that degrade the quality of life in the long run. Remembering that people and their technologies are a part of the natural world may make it possible to imitate the best workings of biological ecosystems and construct artificial ones that can be sustained over the long term.

Strategies for Sustainable Economic Development

World economies are depleting stocks of ecological capital faster than the stocks can be replenished. Yet economic growth can be reconciled with the integrity of the environment.

. . .

Jim MacNeill

Since 1900, the number of people inhabiting the earth has multiplied more than three times. The world economy has expanded 20 times. The consumption of fossil fuels has grown by a factor of 30, and industrial production has increased by a factor of 50; four fifths of that increase has occurred since 1950. This scale of development has produced a world with new realities, realities that have not yet been reflected in human behavior, economics, politics or institutions of government.

The gains in human welfare made possible by this development have been breathtaking, and the potential for future gains is even more awesome. But many of the processes of development that produced these gains are degrading the planet's environment and depleting its basic ecological capital at an alarming rate, leaving increasing numbers of people poor and vulnerable. A decade after the landmark Stockholm Conference on the Human Environment, which was held in 1972, governments began to recognize that environmental destruction at a pace and scale never experienced before was undermining prospects for economic

development and threatening the very survival of the earth's inhabitants.

Is there any way to meet the needs and aspirations of the five billion people now living on the earth without compromising the ability of tomorrow's eight to 10 billion to meet theirs? That, I believe, was the tacit question the United Nations General Assembly sought to answer when in 1983 it called for the establishment of a special, independent commission. The World Commission on Environment and Development, as it was later named, included 23 commissioners from 22 different countries, regionally balanced, including all the major power groups and with a strong majority from developing countries. Gro Harlem Brundtland, who was then Leader of the Opposition in Norway and is now the country's Prime Minister, chaired the commission; Mansour Khalid, a former foreign minister of the Sudan, was vice-chairman. I became secretary general and member (ex officio) and was responsible for directing and managing what became a global enquiry into the state of the world.

The commission went through a broad process of

analysis, learning and debate. We contracted papers, established panels and invited world figures to meet with us. We also did something that no other international commission has attempted: we organized open public hearings in every region of the world, from Jakarta to Moscow, São Paulo to Oslo, Harare to Ottawa. We met and took evidence from nearly a thousand experts, political leaders and concerned citizens on five continents. In the process, we learned firsthand of the contradictions between the reality of environment and development—totally interlocked in the daily lives of people, communities and industries—and the artificial distinctions drawn between the two by academic, economic and political institutions.

In October, 1987, after three years of intensive work, the commission presented its report, "Our Common Future," to the General Assembly. Its answer to the Assembly's tacit question was a heavily conditioned "yes." The needs and aspirations of today could be reconciled with those of tomorrow, providing there are fundamental changes in the way nations manage the world's economy. While this article draws heavily on the commission's report, it reflects my own interpretation, as well as events since 1987 and information that has become available in the past two years.

D uring its three years of work, the commission returned constantly to what I call the "sustainability question": Can growth on the scale projected over the next one to five decades be managed on a basis that is sustainable, both economically and ecologically?

The answer is not evident, since the obstacles to sustainability are mainly social, institutional and political. Economic and ecological sustainability are still dealt with as two separate questions in all governments and international organizations, where they are the responsibility of separate agencies such as ministries of finance and departments of environment. But economic and ecological systems are in fact interlocked. Global warming is a form of feedback from the earth's ecological system to the world's economic system. So are the ozone hole, acid rain in Europe and eastern North America, soil degradation in the prairies, deforestation and species loss in the Amazon, and many other environmental phenomena.

A number of communities and regions have already crossed critical thresholds. In the case of the ozone shield and climatic change, the world as a whole may be on the verge of doing the same. Even so, the most urgent imperative of the next few decades is further rapid growth. A fivefold to tenfold increase in economic activity would be required over the next 50 years in order to meet the needs and aspirations of a burgeoning world population, as well as to begin to reduce mass poverty. If such poverty is not reduced significantly and soon, there really is no way to stop the accelerating decline in the planet's stocks of basic capital: its forests, soils, species, fisheries, waters and atmosphere.

A transition to sustainable development during the first part of the next century would require a minimum of 3 percent annual growth in per capita income in developing countries and vigorous policies to achieve greater equity within developing countries and between the industrialized world and developing countries (see box, "Growth, Distribution and Poverty on page 112). Although they have only one quarter of the world's population, industrialized countries consume about 80 percent of the world's goods. With three quarters of the world's population, developing countries command less than one quarter of the world's wealth. And the imbalance is growing steadily worse.

A fivefold to tenfold increase in economic activity translates into a colossal new burden on the ecosphere. Imagine what it means in terms of planetary investment in housing, transport, agriculture and industry. If current forms of development were employed, energy use alone would have to increase by a factor of five just to bring developing countries, with their present populations, up to the levels of consumption now prevailing in the industrialized world. Similar factors can be cited for food, water, shelter and the other essentials of life.

An increase in economic activity by a factor of from five to 10 sounds enormous, but because of the magic of compound interest, it represents annual growth rates of only between 3.2 and 4.7 percent. What government of any country, developed or developing, does not aspire at least to that? Indeed, such rates are hardly enough to keep up with projected population growth in developing countries.

Figure 10.1 PEDESTRIANS AND HIGHWAY in Ivory Coast epitomize the blend of old and new that is typical of developing countries. Not all the hallmarks of economic growth are as obvious; many of the changes that can bring about sustainable development must take place at the institutional level and should include new policies for regulation, subsidization and the division of responsibility.

Growth, Distribution and Poverty

How quickly can a developing country expect to eliminate poverty? The answer will vary from country to country, but much can be learned from a typical case. Consider, for example, a nation in which half the population lives below the poverty line and in which the distribution of household income is as follows: the top one fifth of households have 50 percent of the nation's total income, the next fifth have 20 percent, the next fifth have 14 percent, another fifth have 9 percent and the bottom fifth have 7 percent. This is a fair representation of the situation in many low-income developing countries.

Now consider two scenarios for distributing increases in income; one in which 25 percent of the incremental income of the richest one fifth is redistributed equally to rest of the population and one in which there is no redistribution. For those two cases, the number of years required to bring poverty down from 50 to 10 percent will be between 18 and 24 years if per capita income grows at 3 percent a year, to between 51 and 70 years if it grows at only 1 percent a year.

Thus, if per capita income grows at 1 percent a year, the time required to eliminate absolute poverty will stretch well into the next century, with or without redistribution of income. To assure that the world is well on its way to sustainable development during the first part of the next century, a minimum of 3 percent annual per capita income growth will be necessary, as well as greater equity in income distribution within developing countries.

Given population trends, per capita income growth of 3 percent a year would require overall national income growth of around 5 percent a year in the developing countries of Asia, 5.5 percent in Latin America and 6 percent in Africa and West Asia. During the 1960's and 1970's, many countries in these regions experienced growth of this magnitude.

Yet during the 1980's, growth in most developing countries came close to a halt. They faced debilitating domestic problems that were not just economic but also ecological and political. And, in many cases, there are clear connections among them. Population growth continued to outstrip economic growth in most developing countries, and two thirds of them suffered falls in per capita income, some as great as 25 percent. Deteriorating terms of trade, such as unstable commodity prices and growing protectionism in developed market economies, and stagnating flows of aid combined to force attention to short-term crises rather than long-term development.

The major problem, particularly in Africa and Latin America, was and still is the debt (see Figure 10.2). The cumulative debt of developing countries has now reached roughly $1 trillion; the interest payments amount to $60 billion a year. The traditional net flow of capital from the industrialized to the developing countries was reversed in 1982: more than $43 billion annually is now transferred in the other direction. And that is only what the World Bank counts.

In addition, today's trading patterns effect a massive transfer of the environmental costs of global gross national product to the poorer, resource-based economies of the developing countries. A study conducted for the commission estimated these costs at about $14 billion a year—more than one third of the total amount of development assistance flowing annually in the other direction. And that $14 billion is a low estimate, because it only includes costs related to environmental pollution and not those related to resource depletion.

Most developing countries, and large parts of many industrialized countries, have resource-based economies (see Figure 10.3). Their economic capital consists mainly of their stocks of environmental resources: their soils, forests, fisheries, species, waters and parks. Their long-term economic development depends on maintaining, if not increasing, these stocks and on enhancing their ability to support agriculture, forestry, fishing, mining and tourism for local use and export.

During the past two decades, the poorer countries of the developing world have experienced a massive depletion of this capital. Just 40 years ago Ethiopia, for example, had a 30 percent forest cover; 12 years

LONG-TERM DEBT AND FINANCIAL FLOWS IN DEVELOPING COUNTRIES FROM 1983 TO 1988 (BILLIONS OF DOLLARS)							
	1982	1983	1984	1985	1986	1987	1988
Debt Disbursed and Outstanding	562.5	644.9	686.7	793.7	893.8	996.3	1020
Debt Service	98.7	92.6	101.8	112.2	116.5	124.9	131
Principal Payments	49.7	45.4	48.6	56.4	61.5	70.9	72
Interest Payments	48.9	47.3	53.2	55.8	54.9	54	59
Net Flows	67.2	51.8	43	32.9	26.2	15.8	16
Net Transfers	**18.2**	**4.6**	**-10.2**	**-22.9**	**-28.7**	**-38.1**	**-43**

Figure 10.2 DEBT AND FINANCIAL FLOWS reflect the worsening financial situation of developing countries. The cumulative debt of developing countries is growing, having now reached more than $1 trillion, and beginning in 1984 the traditional net flow of capital reversed itself: in 1988 $43 billion was transferred from developing countries to developed ones. (Figures supplied by the World Bank.

ago it was down to 4 percent, and today it may be 1 percent. Until this century, India's forests covered more than half of the country. Today they are down to 14 percent and are going fast. In the tropics, 10 trees are being cut for every one planted; in Africa, the ratio is 29 to one. Forest areas nearly equal to the size of the United Kingdom are disappearing every year. Brazil alone may be losing more than eight million hectares annually.

An area larger than the African continent and inhabited by more than one billion people is now at risk from desertification, and every year deserts grow by six million hectares. The WorldWatch Institute estimates yearly topsoil loss at 25 billion tons — roughly the amount that covers Australia's wheatlands. Water use has doubled at least twice in this century and could double again over the next two decades. Yet in 80 developing countries having 40 percent of the world's population, water is already a serious constraint on development.

The basic economic capital of developing, and parts of some developed, countries — their environment and renewable resources — is being consumed faster than it can be restored or replaced. Some developing countries have depleted virtually all of their ecological capital and are on the brink of environmental bankruptcy. The consequences include not only increased hunger and death but also social instability and conflict, as resource depletion and degradation drives millions of environmental refugees across national borders.

With these factors as a backdrop, it is easy to envision the future as one of ever-increasing environmental degradation, poverty and hardship among ever-declining resources in an ever more polluted world. That could, of course, be the outcome of many current development policies and trends, but it is not inevitable (see Figure 10.4).

The commission preferred instead to emphasize the possibility of a "new era of growth" — not the type of growth that dominates today but sustainable growth, growth based on forms and processes of development that do not undermine the integrity of the environment on which they depend. The commission defined sustainable development as consisting of new paths of economic and social progress that "meet the needs of the present without compromising the ability of future generations to meet their own needs."

The concept of sustainable development is not new. As William D. Ruckelshaus points out in Chapter 11, "Toward a Sustainable World," "sustainability is the original economy of the species." Modern civilization, however, has been characterized by unsustainable development, employing forms of decision making that systematically discount the future. Can modern economies be restructured against the criteria of sustainability? This is not an academic question. It is probably a question of survival.

Such restructuring would require changes in societal values and goals, changes in incentives and changes in the dominant processes of decision making. A number of conditions will have to be met in order to make development sustainable. I have already mentioned a few: reviving growth, addressing equity and meeting essential needs and aspirations. Several others are equally important.

One is reducing rates of population growth. The issue is not simply one of numbers. A child born in a rich, industrialized country, where per capita consumption of energy and materials is high, places a much greater burden on the planet than a child born in a poor country. The industrialized world has found that development is the best means of population control. Accompanied by urbanization, rising income levels, improved education and the empowerment of women, development has even brought about negative rates of population growth in countries such as West Germany and Sweden.

Similar processes are at work in some developing countries. In addition, many developing countries are beginning to take strong direct measures to bolster social, cultural and economic motives for couples to have small families. Through family-planning programs, they are also providing to all those who want them the education, technological means and services required to control family size. These efforts require much greater research, financial and especially political support from industrialized countries than they have been getting.

Another essential condition for sustainable development is that a community's and a nation's basic stock of ecological capital should not decrease over time. A constant or increasing stock of natural capital is needed not only to meet the needs of present generations but also to ensure a minimum degree of fairness and equity for future generations.

Can the world's expanding economies begin to live off the interest of the earth's stock of renewable resources, without encroaching on its capital? At the moment, world economies are moving backward at an accelerating pace, but the question remains open. If the annual draw on the earth's stock of renewable resources is to be brought within the capacity of natural systems to generate it, the industrialized world will need to increase by several orders of magnitude its support for strategies aimed at abating pollution, at protecting and preserving essential resource capital and at restoring and rehabilitating assets that have already been depleted or exhausted.

It is much more important, however, to reform the public policies that actively if unintentionally encourage deforestation, desertification, destruction of habitat and species, and decline of air and water quality. These policies and the often enormous budgets they command are much more powerful than any conceivable measures to protect environments or to restore and rehabilitate those already damaged. Unless and until such policies are reformed, nations will not be able to keep up, let alone catch up, with the increasing rates of depletion of their natural capital.

Take agriculture, for example. Agricultural subsidies provide one of the best examples of unwittingly destructive economic policies. Virtually the entire food cycle in North America, Western Europe and Japan attracts huge direct or indirect subsidies. These subsidies encourage farmers to occupy marginal lands and to clear forests and woodlands. They induce farmers to use excessive amounts of pesticides and fertilizers and to waste underground and surface waters in irrigation. Canadian farmers alone lose well over $1 billion a year from reduced production due to erosion stemming from practices underwritten by the Canadian taxpayer.

According to the Organization for Economic Cooperation and Development (OECD) and other sources, the farm-subsidy structure now costs Western governments in excess of $300 billion a year. What conservation programs can compete with that? These subsidies send farmers far more powerful signals than do the small grants usually provided for soil and water conservation.

The adverse effects of these subsidies extend beyond national borders. By generating vast surpluses at great economic and ecological cost, the subsidies create political pressures for still more subsidies: to increase exports, to donate food as nonemergency assistance to developing countries and to raise trade barriers against imported food products. All these measures hurt agricultural productivity.

During the next few decades, agricultural production must be shifted from developed to developing countries, where the growing demand is. Land and price reform is helping to encourage farming in some countries in Asia, Africa and Latin America, but those efforts could easily be undermined by the competitive dumping of Western surpluses. Governments of developing countries are seldom able to resist subsidized or nonemergency food aid. Apart from relieving an ever-present and pressing need,

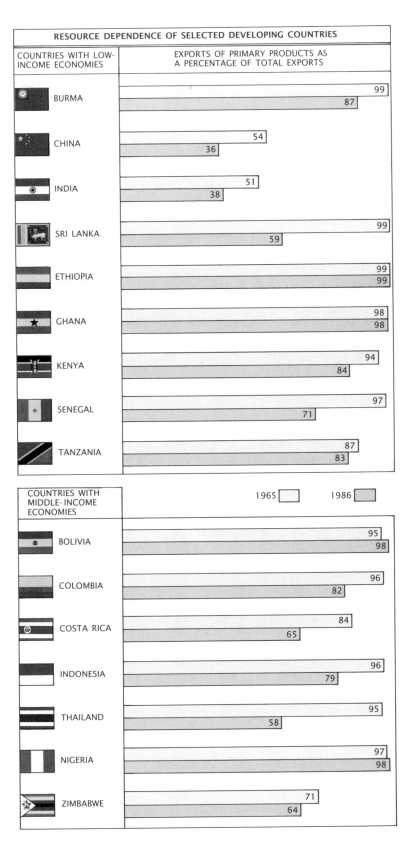

Figure 10.3 RESOURCE DEPEN-DENCE of the economies of selected developing countries is apparent in the percentage of their total exports that are "primary products": fuels, minerals, metals and agricultural products. In many cases the percentage has fallen over the past two decades as resources have been depleted. (Figures from the World Bank 1988 World Development Report.

food shipments reduce the political pressures on governments to reform their own agricultural policies, many of which are equally perverse. It is their farmers who bear most of the brunt of the resulting inaction. Even the most efficient are unable to compete with surpluses dumped at subsidized prices.

These policies are not sustainable. Instead of providing nonemergency "aid" in the form of agricultural surpluses, developed countries should supply financial assistance in ways that encourage and support essential domestic reforms that in turn would increase production and reverse accelerating degradation of the resource base in developing countries. Agricultural and related trade policies in developed countries can also be redesigned and agricultural budgets, national and international, redeployed in ways that not only maintain farm income —which is vital for sustainable agriculture—but also encourage farmers to adopt practices that enhance, rather than deplete, the soil and water base. North American models for such policies go back to the 1930's, when the Soil Conservation Service in the U.S. and the Prairie Farm Rehabilitation Administration in Canada brought the Dust Bowl under control. The 1985 U.S. Food Security Act is a more recent example of the type of changes needed.

Government policies in developed and developing countries similarly abound in incentives to overcut the world's forests. The Brazilian taxpayer underwrites the destruction of the Amazon forests, just as the American taxpayer may be about to underwrite the clearing of the Tongass, the great rain forest of Alaska. Perverse incentives that encourage the overharvesting of temperate as well as tropical forests also mark world trade in forest products. If these policies and incentives remain in place, most of the world's remaining forests will probably be destroyed, with all that implies for food security, desertification, flooding and global warming.

Yet another essential condition for sustainable development concerns the nature of production. If growth rates of up to 3 or 4 percent in the industrialized countries and up to 5 or 6 percent in developing countries are to be sustained, a significant and rapid reduction in the energy and raw-material content of every unit of production will be necessary.

During the past two decades, economic and technological changes have resulted in a leveling off of, or an absolute reduction in, the demand for energy and some basic materials per unit of product. The link between growth and its impact on the environment has also been severed. Nowhere has this been more marked than in energy. Following the first oil shock, between 1973 and 1983, the 24 OECD members, all industrialized nations, improved their energy productivity on average by 1.3 percent annually. Prior to the last oil shock, when prices fell sharply, some countries, including Japan and Sweden, had reached increases in productivity of more than 2 percent a year. The same trends are evident in many other areas, such as water, steel, aluminum, cement and certain chemicals.

The transition to recycled materials is an integral part of limiting the material content of growth, and this transition is already well under way in some countries. In the decade up to 1985, Austria, West Germany, Japan, Sweden and some other countries made significant gains in recycling aluminum, steel, paper and glass. The potential gains remain enormous, however, if only because most countries and industries have a long way to go just to catch up with the leaders. If Canada, for example, were to recycle its newspapers at the Japanese level, it could save 80 million trees a year—approximately 40,000 hectares of forest land.

When an industry reduces the energy and material content of its product, it saves on overall costs per unit of production and reduces environmental emissions and wastes as well. In fact, this is often a more effective way of reducing emissions than expensive "end of pipe" technologies that serve no other purpose. The environmental benefits of resource reduction and recycling extend back to the beginning of the production cycle. They manifest themselves in decreased mining and mining wastes, decreased consumption and pollution of water, decreased air pollution, decreased deforestation and decreased erosion.

Increased energy productivity of from 1 to 2 percent a year could give a reprieve on global warming and bring about major reductions in acid rain. Nations could easily achieve such gains in energy productivity if they would pursue pricing and other policies to encourage efficiency with the same vigor they display in developing conventional sources of supply. And they could do it without sacrificing macroeconomic performance. In fact, the countries that have already made considerable progress in this direction are at the top of the international list of economic performers. Between 1973 and 1984, the energy and raw-material content of a unit of Japanese production dropped by 40 percent. Swe-

Figure 10.4 GANGES RIVER suffers the fate of many natural resources: it has become polluted as a result of economic policies that sacrifice the environment for the sake of development. The government of India has launched a program to restore the Ganges.

den, West Germany and some other countries did as well or better. Increasing the energy and resource efficiency of industrial plants or communities adds up to increasing the efficiency and competitiveness of the national economy.

Developing countries too cannot ignore the implications of lagging behind in energy, resource and environmental productivity. There, as in industrialized countries, increased productivity is critical to sustaining growth, curbing pollution and maintaining competitiveness in the international marketplace. The developed market economies must continue to lead the way in energy and resource reduction and materials recycling, but developing countries must be quick to follow. Moreover, they

must eschew older, more wasteful and inefficient technologies in favor of more advanced ones.

Some newly industrializing countries, such as Taiwan, South Korea and Brazil, are discovering this and are beginning to incorporate state-of-the-art technologies and processes in their industrial structures. Industrialized countries could deploy many policies, particularly policies of trade and aid, to actively promote the transfer to developing countries of advanced industrial processes and technologies that are more energy- and resource-efficient, less polluting and therefore more economically competitive.

Some of the changes required in governmental approaches to energy provide a flavor of those required more generally to reduce the resource and material content of growth. In order to make steady gains in energy efficiency, for example, governments will have to institute politically difficult changes in at least three areas. First, countries will have to consider "conservation pricing," that is, taxing energy during periods of low real prices to encourage increases in productivity. Second, stricter regulations should demand steady improvement in the efficiency of appliances and technologies, from electrical motors to air conditioners, and in building design, automobiles and transportation systems. Third, institutional innovation will be necessary to break utility-supply monopolies and to reorganize the energy sector so that energy services can be sold on a competitive, least-cost basis.

Demand reduction through energy efficiency would buy time to develop renewable energy sources, including substitutes for fuelwood in developing countries. Solar electricity, wind power, mini-hydroturbines, the recycling of waste biomass and the deployment of biomass digestors for making gas and liquid fuel are a few of the many renewable technologies that have enormous potential. Realizing that potential, however, will require a significant shift in research and development from conventional energy sources to new ones.

Once again, current subsidy structures often promote the opposite of what is needed for a sustainable energy future. They ignore the costs of depleting resources and of sullying air, land and water, they favor waste and inefficiency and they underwrite traditional sources of power—coal, oil and nuclear—rather than renewables. In doing so, they impose enormous burdens on already tight budgets and on scarce reserves of foreign currency.

Governments should examine hidden and overt subsidies and reform those that penalize conservation and end-use efficiency. They should also excise policies that retard the development of new and renewable energy resources, particularly those that serve as substitutes for fuelwood. Given the proper incentives, industry itself could play a more effective role.

The most important condition for sustainable development is that environment and economics be merged in decision making. Our economic and ecological systems have become totally interlocked in the real world, but they remain almost totally divorced in our institutions.

During the 1960's and 1970's, governments in more than 100 countries, developed and developing alike, established special environmental-protection and resource-management agencies. But these agencies were hamstrung by limited mandates, limited budgets and little or no political clout. Meanwhile, governments failed to make their powerful central economic and sectoral agencies responsible for the environmental implications of their own policies and expenditures. The resulting balance of forces was grossly unequal. Environmental agencies had about as much chance as a small-town runner, with no training and no financial backing, trying to win a race against Carl Lewis. Despite good intentions, great effort and several leaps forward, they fell further and further behind.

Environmental agencies must be given more capacity and more power to cope with the effects of unsustainable development policies. More important, governments must make their central economic, trade and sectoral agencies directly responsible and accountable for formulating policies and budgets to encourage development that is sustainable. Only then will the ecological dimensions of policy be considered at the same time as the economic, trade, energy, agricultural and other dimensions—on the same agendas and in the same national and international institutions.

One area in which the merging of environmental considerations with economic decision making could have an impact is market incentives. The market is the most powerful instrument available for driving development, and whether or not it encourages and supports sustainable or unsustainable forms of development is largely a function of policy.

As I have already mentioned, government intervention often distorts the market in ways that preordain unsustainable development. Tax and fiscal incentives, pricing and marketing policies and exchange-rate and trade-protection policies all influence the environment and the resource content of the growth that takes place. Yet the people responsible for setting these policies seldom consider their impact on the environment or on stocks of resource capital. When policymakers do take these things into account, they often assume implicitly that the resources are inexhaustible or that substitutes will be found before they become exhausted or that the environment "should" subsidize the market. The same is true of certain sectoral policies, such as the misguided food and energy subsidies that I have already cited.

It is surprising how few government and corporate leaders are aware of the ecologically and economically perverse nature of the incentive systems created by these policies and the often enormous budgets they command. Even the environmental movement is only dimly aware of it. Environmentalists have historically focused on the effects of economic development on health, property and ecosystems. Rarely have they addressed the policies behind such development.

A nation's annual budget establishes the framework of economic and fiscal incentives and disincentives within which corporate leaders, businessmen, farmers and consumers make decisions. It is perhaps the most important environmental policy statement that any government makes in any year, because in their aggregate these decisions serve to enhance or degrade the nation's environment and to increase or reduce its stocks of ecological capital.

A budget that levied taxes on energy, resources and pollution, matched by an equivalent reduction in labor, corporate and value-added taxes, could have a significant effect on consumption patterns and on the cost structure of industry without adding to the overall tax burden on industry and society. Reform of tax systems along such lines seems essential to encourage a transition to sustainable development.

With increased awareness, the politics of changing incentive systems should not be insurmountable. Some leaders of the most advanced industries have welcomed analyses linking economic incentives and environmental integrity. Provided their income is not jeopardized, farmers have everything to gain from incentive systems that encourage practices that maintain or enhance their soil, wood, water and other farm capital. For consumers, many such shifts in incentives would be neutral, and the impact on employment could even be positive.

Reforming tax and incentive systems, though crucial, will not be sufficient. The market is limited in several ways, the most important one being that it cannot take into account the external environmental costs associated with producing, consuming and disposing of goods and services. The market treats the resources of the atmosphere, the oceans and the other commons as free goods. It "externalizes," or transfers to the broader community, the costs of air, water, land and noise pollution and of resource depletion. The broader community shoulders the costs in the form of damages to health, property and ecosystems.

Internalizing these costs again requires government intervention. One attempt was the so-called Polluter Pays Principle (PPP), introduced by member countries of the OECD in 1972. The PPP re-

quires that industries pay the full costs of protecting the environment from the pollution resulting from their activities. It is important mainly because it has the potential to cause the environmental costs of development to be reflected in the prices that consumers pay for goods, thereby biasing consumer choice in favor of those goods whose production, use and disposal have the least impact on the environment. Unfortunately, governments have been notoriously slow to apply the principle, perhaps because it affects consumer prices. Another reason, no doubt, has been pressure from industry. Although as a rule industry is a strong advocate of the market, in this instance it has usually marshalled its forces against it.

Internalizing environmental costs in prices is one way of trying to represent the real costs of development in economic decision making. Integrating resource accounts in national economic accounting systems is another. At the moment, these systems are concerned mainly with the flow of economic activity. Changes in stocks of ecological capital are largely ignored. Integrating the two would enable governments to determine whether reported 3, 5 or 7 percent increases in the gross domestic product are real or whether they reflect instead corresponding or even greater declines in stocks of soils, forests, fisheries, waters, parks and historic places.

With this information, finance ministries and treasuries could get not only a more accurate picture of economic performance but also some idea of the way economic policies are affecting ecological systems. Basic work on resource accounting and on mixed-accounting frameworks has been done in France, Norway, Canada, the U.S. and some other countries. The OECD and a number of independent institutes are currently involved in advancing this work, and some institutes in developing countries have expressed a keen interest in it.

With the gradual integration of the environment in economic decision making, budgets for energy, agriculture and other sectors should begin to include funds to cover the environmental costs of their respective activities. Eventually, the burden of financing sustainable development should be assumed by such budgets. In the interim, sustainable development will demand large sources of new financing.

Developing countries, in particular, will need a significant increase in financial support. In 1988, the WorldWatch Institute attempted some rough estimates of the additional expenditures that would be

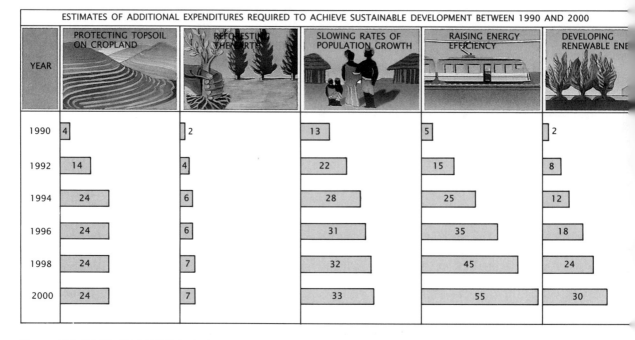

	PROTECTING TOPSOIL ON CROPLAND	REFORESTING THE EARTH	SLOWING RATES OF POPULATION GROWTH	RAISING ENERGY EFFICIENCY	DEVELOPING RENEWABLE ENE
YEAR					
1990	4	2	13	5	2
1992	14	4	22	15	8
1994	24	6	28	25	12
1996	24	6	31	35	18
1998	24	7	32	45	24
2000	24	7	33	55	30

ESTIMATES OF ADDITIONAL EXPENDITURES REQUIRED TO ACHIEVE SUSTAINABLE DEVELOPMENT BETWEEN 1990 AND 2000

Figure 10.5 COST OF ACHIEVING SUSTAINABLE DEVELOPMENT in 10 years, estimated by the WorldWatch Institute, includes expenditures to reduce rates of population growth and to restore and maintain global resources. The figures should be weighed against the world's military expenditures, which alone total close to $1 trillion a year.

required to meet certain targets it deemed essential for global sustainable development by the year 2000. The targets included slowing population growth, protecting topsoil on cropland, reforesting the earth, raising energy efficiency, developing renewable energy and retiring the debt of developing countries (see Figure 10.5).

The institute estimated that those targets could be achieved with annual expenditures approaching $46 billion by 1990 and increasing to $145 billion in 1994 and $150 billion in 2000. A huge political effort would be necessary to raise expenditures to these orders of magnitude. The size of the effort can be judged, perhaps, by the amount of money governments have given to the United Nations Environment Program's Environment Fund since it was established at the 1972 Stockholm Conference: just $30 million a year and often less. At this year's meeting of the UNEP Governing Council, governments agreed only to consider increasing the fund to $100 million. They have a long way to go.

The debt remains the most urgent problem facing developing countries, particularly those in Africa and Latin America. It must be resolved before those countries can be expected to turn their attention to the pressing agenda of poverty and interlocked economic and ecological decline. At last year's meeting in Berlin of the World Bank and the International Monetary Fund (IMF), more countries than ever before seemed to be on the verge of recognizing that the debt situation is untenable. Although several plans for debt relief (most recently the U.S. Brady Plan) have been advanced, they all share two dubious characteristics: the types of measures normally attached as a condition for additional loans and the absence of any programs to sustain, let alone build up, the environmental resource capital of developing countries.

The strict conditionality imposed by the World Bank and the IMF has often appeared to take little account of the social and other consequences of the economic and fiscal measures required. In particular, structural-adjustment programs, as such measures are known, have taken no account of their potential impact on the environment and ecological resources of the country concerned. Measures to reduce budgetary deficits often have a disproportionate impact on such resources. With little else to fall back on, resource-based economies have to draw down their ecological capital even faster than

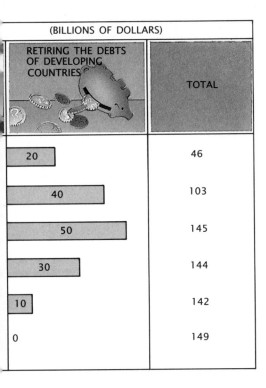

(BILLIONS OF DOLLARS)	
RETIRING THE DEBTS OF DEVELOPING COUNTRIES	TOTAL
20	46
40	103
50	145
30	144
10	142
0	149

they would otherwise in order to earn the foreign currency required for debt repayment. Programs to restore the productive capacity of depleted environments and to preserve habitats, gene pools and tourist areas from destruction are cut back or are simply not implemented. Policies requiring industry and local government to introduce pollution-control measures and programs aimed at providing clean water, sewerage and sanitary facilities are similarly dropped or not implemented.

A recent study by the World Bank confirms that structural-adjustment programs are not neutral in their implications for environmental resources. More significantly, the study argues that it is possible to design such programs so that they have positive, rather than negative, consequences for the nation's environment. Until that happens, the environmental consequences of structural adjustment will continue to be a matter of concern. A number of countries have instructed their representatives on the boards of the IMF and the World Bank to require that the environmental implications of their programs be integrated into background studies for all projects and also into the negotiations for program implementation.

Marshalling sufficient investment for sustainable development will require new initiatives. The World Resources Institute is currently conducting a study of the feasibility of a special international conservation banking program or facility linked to the World Bank. Such a facility could provide loans and facilitate joint financing arrangements for the protection and sustainable development of critical habitats and ecosystems, including those of international significance. There are also several possible international sources of revenue that could be tapped to finance action in support of sustainable development. For example, the use of the international commons or trade in certain commodities could be taxed. This may seem politically unrealistic at present, but global trends have been known to change political realities. In fact, something like that may already be happening.

In June, 1988, at the world conference on the atmosphere held in Toronto and hosted by the Canadian government, the conference participants called on governments to establish a World Atmosphere Fund that would be financed, in part, by a "climate protection" tax. Revenues would come from a levy on the fossil-fuel consumption of industrialized countries, and the proceeds would go to developing countries to help them to limit and adapt to the consequences of global warming and sea-level rise. Others have proposed that the tax should be related to the carbon content of fuels. Most recently, the Norwegian government proposed that, as a starting point, industrialized countries allocate .1 percent of their gross national product to such a fund. The recent Netherlands budget included provision for an annual contribution of 250 million guilders for a global-climate fund, and the government is currently assessing various options for financing and managing such a fund in preparation for an international conference in the Hague this fall.

Military expenditures also represent an enormous pool of capital, human skills and resources. Nations spend nearly $1 trillion a year on military security—more than $2.7 billion a day. Developing countries have increased their arms budgets fivefold in the past 20 years. Some are spending more on their military than they are on education, health, welfare and the environment combined.

A large proportion of these expenditures could well be shifted to more productive purposes. That would require a greater awareness of the growing scale of environmental threats to national and regional security, an awareness that some major political leaders are beginning to voice. It would also require a new and broader concept of security, a concept that encompasses environmental as well as economic and political security. With a broader approach, nations would begin to find many instances in which their security could be improved more effectively through expenditures to protect, preserve and restore basic environmental capital assets than through expenditures for arms.

The possibility of nuclear war undoubtedly represents the gravest potential danger to environmental resources, life-support systems and survival. Yet the geopolitical implications of interlocked economic-ecological change are enormous. In parts of the Middle East, Africa, Latin America and Asia, invading deserts, competition for water and the movements of ecological refugees are already significant sources of political unrest and international tension (see Figure 10.6). These situations will only get worse. Climatic change alone will heighten tension as major shifts occur in the national boundaries defined by bodies of water, in centers of urban and

agricultural production and in the numbers of ecological refugees.

Threats to the peace and security of nations and regions from environmental breakdown are potentially greater than any foreseeable military threat from conventional arms. If these threats stemmed from potential military action by unfriendly powers, any nation or group of nations would respond with a massive mobilization of diplomatic, military and other resources. Yet, faced with a security threat in the form of environmental destruction, nations and the world community seem to be incapable of mounting an effective response.

Countries must begin to treat the integrity of the environment and the sustainability of development as a foreign-policy issue of paramount importance. Measures to reduce debt and to increase the net flow of resources to developing countries should be backed up with coherent policies on aid, on agricultural and other forms of trade, and on the import or export of hazardous chemicals, wastes and technology. A "foreign policy for environment and development" could help to induce greater coherence in these areas. It could also serve to improve overall effectiveness, coordination and cooperation with re-

Figure 10.6 CAMP OF DROUGHT REFUGEES in Upper Volta depicts the plight of millions of people driven from their homes by environmental crises. Such mass movements of populations can create international tension as refugees cross national borders.

gard to rapidly evolving developments concerning the management of the commons—the oceans, the atmosphere, Antarctica and outer space.

There is a rapidly growing potential for conflict over global warming and sea-level rise, the spread of deserts, the allocation of shared water and other resources and other "environmental" issues. Yet, properly approached within the context of promoting sustainable economic development, these issues could force a new spirit of international cooperation as well as fresh thinking about multilateral approaches to other global issues.

Toward a Sustainable World

What policies can lead to the changes in behavior—of individuals, industries and governments—that will allow development and growth to take place within the limits set by ecological imperatives?

. . .

William D. Ruckelshaus

The difficulty of converting scientific findings into political action is a function of the uncertainty of the science and the pain generated by the action. Given the current uncertainties surrounding just one aspect of the global environmental crisis—the predicted rise in greenhouse gases—and the enormous technological and social effort that will be required to control that rise, it is fair to say that responding successfully to the multifaceted crisis will be a difficult political enterprise. It means trying to get a substantial proportion of the world's people to change their behavior in order to (possibly) avert threats that will otherwise (probably) affect a world most of them will not be alive to see.

The models that predict climatic change, for ex- ample, are subject to varying interpretations as to the timing, distribution and severity of the changes in store. Also, whereas models may convince scientists, who understand their assumptions and limitations, as a rule projections make poor politics. It is hard for people—hard even for the groups of people who constitute governments—to change in response to dangers that may not arise for a long time or that just might not happen at all.

How, then, can we make change happen? The previous chapters have documented the reality of the global ecological crisis and have pointed to some specific ameliorative measures. This chapter is about how to shape the policies, launch the programs and harness the resources that will lead to the adoption of such measures—and that will actually convince ordinary people throughout the world to start doing things differently.

Insurance is the way people ordinarily deal with potentially serious contingencies, and it is appropriate here as well. People consider it prudent to pay insurance premiums so that if catastrophe strikes, they or their survivors will be better off than if there had been no insurance. The analogy is clear. Current resources foregone or spent to prevent the

Figure 11.1 SMOKING GUN. A citizen of Nizhniy Tagil, an industrial center near Sverdlovsk in the U.S.S.R., stands on a soot-laden snowbank and contemplates the emission stacks of the local iron and steel mill. In the spring of 1988 a particularly dense smog prompted public demonstrations that led to the closing down of one of the mill's two coke ovens. Smoking chimneys, icons of economic activity, are also symbolic of the impact exerted by the works of human beings on the global ecosystem.

buildup of greenhouse gases are a kind of premium. Moreover, as long as we are going to pay premiums, we might as well pay them in ways that will yield dividends in the form of greater efficiency, improved human health or more widely distributed prosperity. If we turn out to be wrong on greenhouse warming or ozone depletion, we still retain the dividend benefits. In any case, no one complains to the insurance company when disaster does not strike.

That is the argument for some immediate, modest actions. We can hope that if shortages or problems arise, there will turn out to be a technological fix or set of fixes, or that technology and the normal workings of the market will combine to solve the problem by product substitution. Already, for example, new refrigerants that do not have the atmospheric effects of the chlorofluorocarbons are being introduced; perhaps a cheap and nonpolluting source of energy will be discovered.

It is comforting to imagine that we might arrive at a more secure tomorrow with little strain, to suppose with Dickens's Mr. Micawber that something will turn up. Imagining is harmless, but counting on such a rescue is not. We need to face up to the fact that something enormous may be happening to our world. Our species may be pushing up against some immovable limits on the combustion of fossil fuels and damage to ecosystems. We must at least consider the possibility that, besides those modest adjustments for the sake of prudence, we may have to prepare for far more dramatic changes, changes that will begin to shape a sustainable world economy and society.

Sustainability is the nascent doctrine that economic growth and development must take place, and be maintained over time, within the limits set by ecology in the broadest sense—by the interrelations of human beings and their works, the biosphere and the physical and chemical laws that govern it (see Figure 11.2). The doctrine of sustainability holds too that the spread of a reasonable level of prosperity and security to the less developed nations is essential to protecting ecological balance and hence essential to the continued prosperity of the wealthy nations. It follows that environmental protection and economic development are complementary rather than antagonistic processes.

Can we move nations and people in the direction of sustainability? Such a move would be a modification of society comparable in scale to only

Figure 11.2 COEXISTENCE of nature and human activity is celebrated in *Progress*, painted by Asher B. Durand in 1853. It is an image in which a "balanced reconciliation of

two other changes: the agricultural revolution of the late Neolithic and the Industrial Revolution of the past two centuries. Those revolutions were gradual, spontaneous and largely unconscious. This one will have to be a fully conscious operation, guided by the best foresight that science can provide—foresight pushed to its limit. If we actually do it, the undertaking will be absolutely unique in humanity's stay on the earth.

The shape of this undertaking cannot be clearly seen from where we now stand. The conventional image is that of a crossroads: a forced choice of one direction or another that determines the future for

nature and culture seems to have been achieved," according to the art historian Barbara Novak. Durand's 19th-century view of industrialization might well serve as a metaphor for today's vision of sustainable development. (Painting is in the Warner Collection of the Gulf States Paper Corporation, in Tuscaloosa, Ala.)

some appreciable period. But this does not at all capture the complexity of the current situation. A more appropriate image would be that of a canoeist shooting the rapids: survival depends on continually responding to information by correct steering. In this case the information is supplied by science and economic events; the steering is the work of policy, both governmental and private.

Taking control of the future therefore means tightening the connection between science and policy. We need to understand where the rocks are in time to steer around them. Yet we will not devote the appropriate level of resources to science or ac-

cept the policies mandated by science unless we do something else. We have to understand that we are all in the same canoe and that steering toward sustainability is necessary.

Sustainability was the original economy of our species. Preindustrial peoples lived sustainably because they had to; if they did not, if they expanded their populations beyond the available resource base, then sooner or later they starved or had to migrate. The sustainability of their way of life was maintained by a particular consciousness regarding nature: the people were spiritually connected to the animals and plants on which they subsisted; they were part of the landscape, or of nature, not set apart as masters.

The era of this "original sustainability" eventually came to an end. The development of cities and the maintenance of urban populations called for intensive agriculture yielding a surplus. As a population grows, it requires an expansion of production, either by conquest or colonization or improved technique. A different consciousness, also embodied in a structure of myth, sustains this mode of life. The earth and its creatures are considered the property of humankind, a gift from the supernatural. Man stands outside of nature, which is a passive playing field that he dominates, controls and manipulates. Eventually, with industrialization, even the past is colonized: the forests of the Carboniferous are mined to support ever-expanding populations. Advanced technology gives impetus to the basic assumption that there is essentially no limit to humanity's power over nature.

This consciousness, this condition of "transitional unsustainability," is dominant today. It has two forms. In the underdeveloped, industrializing world, it is represented by the drive to develop at any environmental cost. It includes the wholesale destruction of forests, the replacement of sustainable agriculture by cash crops, the attendant exploitation of vulnerable lands by people such cash cropping forces off good land and the creation of industrial centers that are also centers of environmental pollution.

In the industrialized world, unsustainable development has generated wealth and relative comfort for about one fifth of humankind, and among the populations of the industrialized nations the consciousness supporting the unsustainable economy is nearly universal. With a few important exceptions, the environmental-protection movement in those nations, despite its major achievements in passing legislation and mandating pollution-control measures, has not had a substantial effect on the lives of most people. Environmentalism has been ameliorative and corrective—not a restructuring force. It is encompassed within the consciousness of unsustainability.

Although we cannot return to the sustainable economy of our distant ancestors, in principle there is no reason why we cannot create a sustainability consciousness suitable to the modern era. Such a consciousness would include the following beliefs:

1. *The human species is part of nature. Its existence depends on its ability to draw sustenance from a finite natural world; its continuance depends on its ability to abstain from destroying the natural systems that regenerate this world.* This seems to be the major lesson of the current environmental situation as well as being a direct corollary of the second law of thermodynamics.

2. *Economic activity must account for the environmental costs of production.* Environmental regulation has made a start here, albeit a small one. The market has not even begun to be mobilized to preserve the environment; as a consequence an increasing amount of the "wealth" we create is in a sense stolen from our descendants.

3. *The maintenance of a livable global environment depends on the sustainable development of the entire human family.* If 80 percent of the members of our species are poor, we can not hope to live in a world at peace; if the poor nations attempt to improve their lot by the methods we rich have pioneered, the result will eventually be world ecological damage.

This consciousness will not be attained simply because the arguments for change are good or because the alternatives are unpleasant. Nor will exhortation suffice. The central lesson of realistic policy-making is that most individuals and organizations change when it is in their interest to change, either because they derive some benefit from changing or because they incur sanctions when they do not—and the shorter the time between change (or failure to change) and benefit (or sanction), the better. This is not mere cynicism. Although people will struggle and suffer for long periods to achieve a goal, it is not reasonable to expect people or organizations to work against their immediate interests for very long—particularly in a democratic system, where what they perceive to be their interests are so important in guiding the government.

To change interests, three things are required. First, a clear set of values consistent with the consciousness of sustainability must be articulated by leaders in both the public and the private sector. Next, motivations need to be established that will support the values. Finally, institutions must be developed that will effectively apply the motivations. The first is relatively easy, the second much harder and the third perhaps hardest of all.

Values similar to those I described above have indeed been articulated by political leaders throughout the world. In the past year the president

Figure 11.3 ENVIRONMENTAL ISSUES look different to people and governments in the rich and in the poor na- tions. (Cartoon by Scott Willis of the *San Jose Mercury News*.)

and the secretary of state of the U.S., the leader of the Soviet Union, the prime minister of Great Britain and the presidents of France and Brazil have all made major environmental statements. In July the leaders of the Group of Seven major industrialized nations called for "the early adoption, worldwide, of policies based on sustainable development." Most industrialized nations have a structure of national environmental law that to at least some extent reflects such values, and there is even a small set of international conventions that begin to do the same thing.

Mere acceptance of a changed value structure, although it is a prerequisite, does not generate the required change in consciousness, nor does it change the environment. Although diplomats and lawyers may argue passionately over the form of words, talk is not action. In the U.S., which has a set of environmental statutes second to none in their stringency, and where for the past 15 years poll after poll has recorded the American people's desire for increased environmental protection (see Figure 11.4), the majority of the population participates in the industrialized world's most wasteful and most polluting style of life. The values are there; the ap-

propriate motivations and institutions are patently inadequate or nonexistent.

The difficulties of moving from stated values to actual motivations and institutions stem from basic characteristics of the major industrialized nations— the nations that must, because of their economic strength, preeminence as polluters and dominant share of the world's resources, take the lead in any changing of the present order. These nations are market-system democracies. The difficulties, ironically, are inherent in the free-market economic system on the one hand and in democracy on the other.

The economic problem is the familiar one of externalities: the environmental cost of producing a good or service is not accounted for in the price paid for it. As the economist Kenneth E. Boulding has put it: "All of nature's systems are closed loops, while economic activities are linear and assume inexhaustible resources and 'sinks' in which to throw away our refuse." In willful ignorance, and in violation of the core principle of capitalism, we often refuse to treat environmental resources as capital. We spend them as income and are as befuddled as any profligate heir when our checks start to bounce.

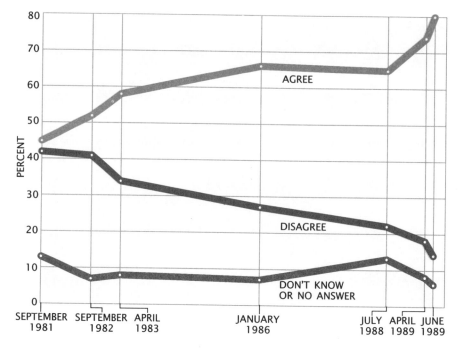

Figure 11.4 ENVIRONMENTAL VALUES have drawn increasing support in the U.S. In *New York Times*/CBS News polls taken since 1981, respondents were asked to react to this statement: "Protecting the environment is so important that requirements and standards cannot be too high, and continuing environmental improvements must be made regardless of cost." The two latest polls were taken after the *Exon Valdez* spill.

Such "commons" as the atmosphere, the seas, fisheries and goods in public ownership are particularly vulnerable to being overspent in this way, treated as either inexhaustible resources or bottomless sinks. The reason is that the incremental benefit to each user accrues exclusively to that user, and in the short term it is a gain. The environmental degradation is spread out among all users and is apparent only in the long term, when the resource shows signs of severe stress or collapse. Some years ago the biologist Garrett Hardin called this the tragedy of the commons.

The way to avoid the tragedy of the commons — to make people pay the full cost of a resource use — is to close the loops in economic systems. The general failure to do this in the industrialized world is related to the second problem, the problem of action in a democracy. Modifying the market to reflect environmental costs is necessarily a function of government. Those adversely affected by such modifications, although they may be a tiny minority of the population, often have disproportionate influence on public policy. In general, the much injured minority proves to be a more formidable lobbyist than the slightly benefited majority .

The Clean Air Act of 1970 in the U.S., arguably the most expensive and far-reaching environmental legislation in the world, is a case in point. Parts of the act were designed not so much to cleanse the air as to protect the jobs of coal miners in high-sulfur coal regions. Utilities and other high-volume consumers were not allowed to substitute low-sulfur coal to meet regulatory requirements but instead had to install scrubbing devices.

Although the act expired seven years ago, Congress found it extraordinarily difficult to develop a revision, largely because of another set of contrary interests involving acid rain. The generalized national interest in reducing the environmental damage attributable to this long-range pollution had to overcome the resistance of both high-sulfur-coal mining interests and the Midwestern utilities that would incur major expenses if they were forced to control sulfur emissions. The problem of conflicting interests is exacerbated by the distance between major sources of acid rain and the regions that suffer the most damage (see Figure 11.5). It is accentuated when the pollution crosses state and national boundaries: elected representatives are less likely to countenance short-term adverse effects on their constituents when the immediate beneficiaries are nonconstituents.

The question, then, is whether the industrial democracies will be able to overcome political constraints on bending the market system toward long-term sustainability. History provides some cause for optimism: a number of contingencies have led nations to accept short-term burdens in order to meet a long-term goal.

War is the obvious example. Things considered politically or economically impossible can be accomplished in a remarkably short time, given the belief that national survival is at stake. World War II mobilized the U.S. population, changed work patterns, manipulated and controlled the price and supply of goods and reorganized the nation's industrial plant.

Another example is the Marshall Plan for reconstructing Europe after World War II. In 1947 the U.S. spent nearly 3 percent of its gross domestic product on this huge set of projects. Although the impetus for the plan came from fear that Soviet influence would expand into Western Europe, the plan did establish a precedent for massive investment in increasing the prosperity of foreign nations.

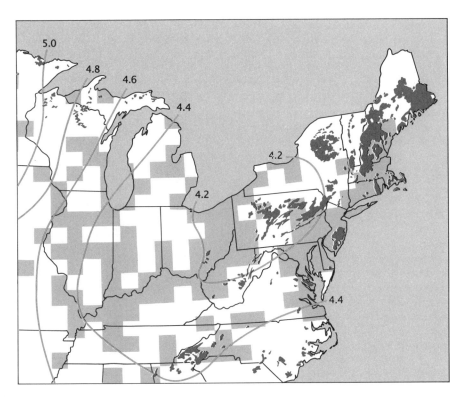

Figure 11.5 ACID RAIN is a political problem because industrial emissions responsible for acidic precipitation cross political borders. Regions where the density of sulfur dioxide emissions was more than 1.5 tons per square kilometer in 1980 are shown in gray; states with the largest emissions are in the Midwest and along the Ohio River. The contours show the pH of precipitation; low pH means high acidity. Within the low-pH regions, lakes and streams are at highest risk of acidification where the water's alkalinity is lowest (orange). (Sulfur dioxide data from the National Acid Precipitation Assessment Program, alkalinity data from James M. Omernick of the Environmental Protection Agency and colleagues.)

There are other examples. Feudalism was abandoned in Japan, as was slavery in the U.S., in the 19th century; this century has seen the retreat of imperialism and the creation of the European Economic Community. In each case important interests gave way to new national goals.

If it is possible to change, how do we begin to motivate change? Clearly, government policy must lead the way, since market prices of commodities typically do not reflect the environmental costs of extracting and replacing them, nor do the prices of energy from fossil fuels reflect the risks of climatic change. Pricing policy is the most direct means of ensuring that the full environmental cost of goods and services is accounted for. When government owns a resource, or supplies it directly, the price charged can be made to reflect the true cost of the product. The market will adjust to this as it does to true scarcity: by product substitution (see Figure 11.6) and conservation.

Environmental regulation should be refocused to mobilize rather than suppress the ingenuity and creativity of industry. For example, additional gains in pollution control should be sought not simply by increasing the stringency or technical specificity of command-and-control regulation but also by implementing incentive-based systems. Such systems magnify public-sector decisions by tens of thousands of individual and corporate decisions. To be sure, incentive systems are not a panacea. For some environmental problems, such as the use of unacceptably dangerous chemicals, definitive regulatory measures will always be required. Effective policies will include a mixture of incentive-based and regulatory approaches.

Yet market-based approaches will be a necessary part of any attempt to reduce the greenhouse effect. Here the most attractive options involve the encouragement of energy efficiency. Improving efficiency meets the double-benefit standard of insurance: it is good in itself, and it combats global warming by reducing carbon dioxide emissions. If the world were to improve energy efficiency by 2 percent a year, the global average temperature could be kept within one degree Celsius of present levels. Many industrialized nations have maintained a rate of improvement close to that over the past 15 years.

Promoting energy efficiency is also relatively painless. The U.S. reduced the energy intensity of its domestic product by 23 percent between 1973

and 1985 without much notice. Substantial improvement in efficiency is available even with existing technology. Something as simple as bringing all U.S. buildings up to the best world standards could save enormous amounts of energy. Right now more energy passes through the windows of buildings in the U.S. than flows through the Alaska pipeline.

Efficiency gains may nevertheless have to be promoted by special market incentives, because energy prices tend to lag behind increases in income. A "climate protection" tax of $1 per million Btu's on coal and 60 cents per million Btu's on oil is an example of such an incentive. It would raise gasoline prices by 11 cents a gallon and the cost of electricity an average of 10 percent, and it would yield $53 billion annually.

Direct regulation by the setting of standards is cumbersome, but it may be necessary when implicit market signals are not effective. Examples are the mileage standards set in the U.S. for automobiles and the efficiency standards for appliances that were adopted in 1986. The appliance standards will

Figure 11.6 SUBSTITUTION is one route to the reduction of pollution. Substitution of methanol (already available at some gas stations in Los Angeles) for gasoline would cut down emissions of nitrogen oxides.

save $28 billion in energy costs by the year 2000 and keep 342 million tons of carbon out of the atmosphere.

Over the long term it is likely that some form of emissions-trading program will be necessary—and on a much larger scale than has been the case heretofore. (Indeed, the President's new Clean Air Act proposal includes a strengthened system of tradeable permits.) In such a program all major emitters of pollutants would be issued permits specifying an allowable emission level. Firms that decide to reduce emissions below the specified level—for example, by investing in efficiency—could sell their excess "pollution rights" to other firms. Those that find it prohibitively costly to retrofit old plants or build new ones could buy such rights or could close down their least efficient plants and sell the unneeded rights.

Another kind of emissions trading might reduce the impact of carbon dioxide emissions (see Figure 11.7). Companies responsible for new greenhouse-gas emissions could be required to offset them by improving overall efficiency or closing down plants, or by planting or preserving forests that would help absorb the emissions. Once the system is established, progress toward further reduction of emissions would be achieved by progressively cranking down the total allowable levels of various pollu-tants, on both a national and a permit-by-permit basis.

The kinds of programs I have just described will need to be supported by research providing a scientific basis for new environmental-protection strategies. Research into safe, nonpolluting energy sources and more energy-efficient technologies would seem to be particularly good bets. An example: in the mid-1970's the U.S. Department of Energy developed a number of improved-efficiency technologies at a cost of $16 million; among them were a design for compact fluorescent lamps that could replace incandescent bulbs, and window coatings that save energy during both heating and cooling seasons. At current rates of implementation, the new technologies should generate $63 billion in energy savings by the year 2010.

The motivation of change toward sustainability will have to go far beyond the reduction of pollution and waste in the developed countries, and it cannot be left entirely to the environmental agencies in those countries. The agencies whose goals are economic development, exploitation of resources and international trade—and indeed foreign policy in general—must also adopt sustainable development as a central goal. This is a formidable challenge, for it touches the heart of numerous special interests. Considerable political skill will be required to achieve for environmental protection the policy pre-

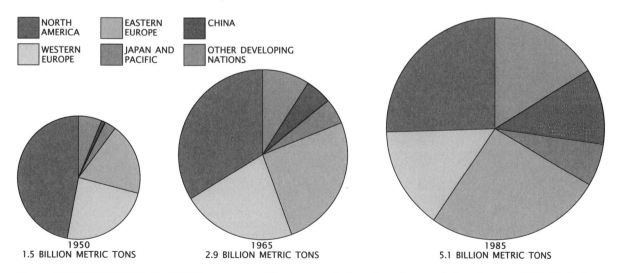

1950
1.5 BILLION METRIC TONS

1965
2.9 BILLION METRIC TONS

1985
5.1 BILLION METRIC TONS

Figure 11.7 DEVELOPED NATIONS are responsible for far more industrial emission of carbon dioxide, a major greenhouse gas, than are the developing nations. Total emissions have increased sharply since 1950. (Data from the World Resources Institute.)

eminence that only economic issues and national security (in the military sense) have commanded.

But it is in relations with the developing world that the industrialized nations will face their greatest challenges (see Figure 11.8). Aid is both an answer and a perpetual problem. Total official development assistance from the developed to the developing world stands at around $35 billion a year. This is not much money. The annual foreign-aid expenditure of the U.S. alone would be $127 billion if it spent the same proportion of its gross national product on foreign aid as it did during the peak years of the Marshall Plan.

There is no point, of course, in even thinking about the adequacy of aid to the undeveloped nations until the debt issue is resolved. The World Bank has reported that in 1988 the 17 most indebted countries paid the industrialized nations and multilateral agencies $31.1 billion more than they received in aid. This obviously cannot go on. Debt-for-nature swapping has taken place between such major lenders as Citicorp and a number of countries in South America: the bank forgives loans in exchange for the placing of land in conservation areas or parks. This is admirable, but it will not in itself solve the problem. Basic international trading relations will have to be redesigned in order to eliminate, among other things, the ill effects on the undeveloped world of agricultural subsidies and tariff barriers in the industrialized world.

A prosperous rural society based on sustainable agriculture must be the prelude to future develop-ment in much of the developing world, and governments there will have to focus on what motivates people to live in an environmentally responsible manner. Farmers will not grow crops when governments subsidize urban populations by keeping prices to farmers low. People will not stop having too many children if the labor of children is the only economic asset they have. Farmers will not improve the land if they do not own it; it is clear that land-tenure reform will have to be instituted.

Negative sanctions against abusing the environment are also missing throughout much of the undeveloped world; to help remedy this situation, substantial amounts of foreign aid could be focused directly on improving the status of the environmental ministries in developing nations. These ministries are typically impoverished and ineffective, particularly in comparison with their countries' economic-development and military ministries. To cite one small example: the game wardens of Tanzania receive an annual salary equivalent to the price paid to poachers for two elephant tusks—one reason the nation has lost two thirds of its elephant population to the ivory trade in the past decade.

To articulate the values and devise the motivations favoring a sustainable world economy, existing institutions will need to change and new ones will have to be established. These will be difficult tasks, because institutions are powerful to the extent that they support powerful interests—which usually implies support of the status quo.

The important international institutions in today's

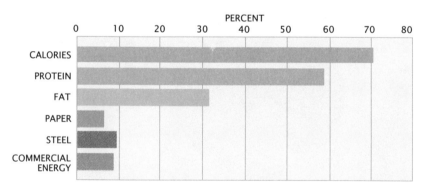

Figure 11.8 DEVELOPED NATIONS consume far more of the world's goods than do the developing nations—which have some 75 percent of the world's population. Per capita consumption in the developing nations is shown as a per-cent of that in the developed nations. (Data are estimates by the World Commission on Environment and Development).

world are those concerned with money, with trade and with national defense. Those who despair of environmental concerns ever reaching a comparable level of importance should remember that current institutions (for example, NATO, the World Bank, multinational corporations) have fairly short histories. They were formed out of pressing concerns about acquiring and expanding wealth and maintaining national sovereignty. If concern for the environment becomes comparably pressing, comparable institutions will be developed.

To further this goal, three things are wanted. The first is money. The annual budget of the United Nations Environment Program (UNEP) is $30 million, a derisory amount considering its responsibilities. If nations are serious about sustainability, they will provide this central environmental organization with serious money, preferably money derived from an independent source in order to reduce its political vulnerability. A tax on certain uses of common world resources has been suggested as a means to this end.

The second thing wanted is information. We require strong international institutions to collect, analyze and report on environmental trends and risks. The Earthwatch program run by the UNEP is a beginning, but there is need for an authoritative source of scientific information and advice that is independent of national governments. There are many nongovernmental or quasi-governmental organizations capable of filling this role; they need to be pulled together into a cooperative network. We need a global institution capable of answering questions of global importance.

The third thing wanted is integration of effort. The world cannot afford a multiplication of conflicting efforts to solve common problems. On the aid front in particular, this can be tragically absurd: Africa alone is currently served by 82 international donors and more than 1,700 private organizations. In 1980, in the tiny African nation Burkina Faso (population about eight million) 340 independent aid projects were under way. We need to form and strengthen coordinating institutions that combine the separate strengths of nongovernmental organizations, international bodies and industrial groups and to focus their efforts on specific problems.

Finally, in creating the consciousness of advanced sustainability, we shall have to redefine our concepts of political and economic feasibility. These concepts are, after all, simply human constructs; they were different in the past, and they will surely change in the future. But the earth is real, and we are obliged by the fact of our utter dependence on it to listen more closely than we have to its messages.

EDITOR'S NOTE

Ruckelshaus acknowledges the major contribution of Michael A. Gruber, a senior policy analyst at the E.P.A., in the preparation of his chapter.

Epilogue

How to secure our common future

. . .

Gro Harlem Brundtland

When the 20th century began, neither human beings nor human technology had the power to radically alter the global ecosystem. Today, as the century draws to a close, human beings in ever-increasing numbers have that power, and as a result of their activity on the planet, major unintended changes are taking place in the atmosphere, the biosphere and the hydrosphere. These changes outstrip our present ability to cope; the world's financial and political institutions are out of step with the workings of nature.

Poverty is a major cause and also a major effect of global environmental problems. It is futile to seek solutions to environmental disturbances without considering them from a broad perspective that encompasses the factors underlying world poverty and the inequalities within and among nations. For developing countries, poverty lies at the heart of all issues. The poor are forced to eat next year's seed corn, to cut scarce forests for fuel-wood. Although such practices may be rational short-term tactics for survival, in the longer term they can only result in disaster.

Yet it is both futile and an insult to the poor to tell them that they must remain in poverty to "protect the environment." The World Commission on Environment and Development concluded in its 1987 report, "Our Common Future," that sustained economic growth, which is a precondition for the elimination of mass poverty, is possible only within a more equitable international economic regime. The commission called for a new era of economic growth—growth that enhances the resource base rather than degrades it. We know now that growth and development need not be environmentally degrading, that in fact growth can create the capital and the capacity necessary to solve environmental problems. And without growth, how can we provide for twice the present population some time in the next century, when we cannot provide for everybody today?

Those of us who live in the industrialized world have an obligation to ensure that international economic relations help rather than hinder the prospects for sustainable development. It is our duty, as well as in our own self-interest, to do so. Commodity prices must be adjusted to provide a fair international distribution of income. Official development-assistance programs and private loans to developing countries, as well as private investment, must be improved, both in quality and in quantity. Policies —both national and international—will have to be changed so that capital transfers are sensitive to environmental impacts and can contribute to long-term sustainability.

Energy is another area of vital importance. As

nations continue to develop they will require more, not less, total energy; their industrialization and rapidly growing populations will depend on it. Yet global energy consumption, even at its present levels, has already created serious environmental woes. How can an increase in energy use be tolerated without further deterioration of the global ecosystem? The solution, we believe, is to place energy-efficiency policies at the cutting edge of national energy strategies, regardless of the relatively low price of such traditional fuels as coal and petroleum.

The commission found no absolute limits to growth. Limits are indeed imposed by the impact of present technologies and social organization on the biosphere, but we have the ingenuity to change. And change we must. The report of the commission offers governments and international institutions an agenda for change. After a period of standstill and even deterioration in global cooperation, the time has come for higher aspirations, for increased political will to address our common future.

The United Nations system with all of its specialized agencies has the capacity to reach our common goals. We call for a fundamental commitment by all governments and institutions to make sustainable development the guiding principle of the international community. To secure our common future, we need a new international vision based on cooperation and a new international ethic based on the realization that the issues with which we wrestle are globally interconnected. This is not only a moral ethic but also a practical one — the only way we can pursue our own self-interests on a small and closely knit planet.

Environment and development have come to the top of the international agenda. Policies to promote sustainable development must be devised by nations both in the Northern and in the Southern Hemisphere, and they must also take into account the imbalances in international economic relations that prevail today.

Our ambition should now be to make the 1990's a decade of rapid social, economic and environmental cooperation rather than confrontation. A global economic consensus for growth should be developed. To be consistent with sustainable development, such a consensus must observe ecological limitations. It should include sound economic policies within developing countries and be particularly sensitive to the poorer nations in Asia, Africa and Latin America.

It is time for a global economic summit. Would it not be timely to consider both our economic and environmental concerns at such a summit, given the critical linkage between the two? The large ecological issues — the greenhouse effect, the disappearing ozone layer and sustainable utilization of tropical forests — are tasks facing humankind as a whole. The World Commission on Environment and Development presented innovative ideas on how to mobilize additional financial resources. The time is now ripe to explore these problems both institutionally and financially.

Our generation is the first one to have seen planet earth from a distance. And from that perspective it is all too apparent that our species is dependent on a single tiny, fragile globe floating in space, a closed and vulnerable system.

The report of the commission offers a challenging agenda. We were asked to offer strategies for the future and to provide motivation for adopting new policies. In demonstrating the real threats to both our present and our future and showing that workable solutions are at hand, our report provides that motivation. We hope that it will ultimately achieve its purpose of generating the debate and discussion that are necessary to revitalize international cooperation.

The Authors

WILLIAM C. CLARK ("Managing Planet Earth") is a senior research associate at Harvard University's Kennedy School of Government. He received a B.S. in 1971 from Yale University and a Ph.D. in 1979 from the University of British Columbia. He is a member of the U.S. National Academy of Sciences Committee on Global Change and edits *Environment* magazine. In 1983 he received the MacArthur Prize.

THOMAS E. GRAEDEL and **PAUL J. CRUTZEN** ("The Changing Atmosphere") are pioneers in the study of atmospheric chemistry. Graedel is Distinguished Member of the technical staff at Bell Laboratories. Crutzen, the co-developer of the "nuclear winter" theory, is director of the air chemistry division of the Max-Planck-Institute for Chemistry in Mainz, West Germany, and a visiting professor at the University of Chicago. In 1989 he received the prestigious Tyler Prize for his contributions to environmental science.

STEPHEN H. SCHNEIDER ("The Changing Climate") is head of the interdisciplinary climate-systems program at the National Center for Atmospheric Research in Boulder, Colo. He received a Ph.D. from Columbia University and has often been a spokesman for climatology.

J. W. MAURITS LA RIVIÈRE ("Threats to the World's Water") is secretary general of the International Council of Scientific Unions and has been a professor of environmental microbiology and chairman of the environmental engineering department at the International Institute for Hydraulic and Environmental Engineering in the Netherlands. After receiving his Ph.D. in microbiology from the Delft University of Technology, he spent a year at Stanford University's Hopkins Marine Station before returning to the Netherlands to join the staff at IHE.

EDWARD O. WILSON ("Threats to Biodiversity") is Frank B. Baird, Jr., Professor of Science and Curator in Entomology at Harvard University. He did his undergraduate studies in evolutionary biology at the University of Alabama and received his Ph.D. in biology from Harvard. He has been awarded the National Medal of Science, the Pulitzer Prize in general nonfiction for his book *On Human Nature* and the Tyler Prize for environmental achievement.

NATHAN KEYFITZ ("The Growing Human Population") received his B.Sc. in 1934 from McGill University and his Ph.D. in sociology from the University of Chicago in 1952. He has held appointments at the University of Toronto, University of Chicago, University of California at Berkeley, Harvard University and Ohio State University. He is currently Andelot Professor Emeritus at Harvard, Lazarus Professor Emeritus at Ohio State, head of the Population Program at the International Institute of Applied Systems Analysis in Austria and a consultant to the government of Indonesia.

PIERRE R. CROSSON and **NORMAN J. ROSENBERG** ("Strategies for Agriculture") are colleagues at Resources for the Future in Washington, D.C. Crosson, who has a Ph.D. in economics from Columbia University, is senior fellow in the Energy and Natural Resources Division. Rosenberg, whose Ph.D. in soil physics and meteorology is from Rutgers University, is director of the Climate Resources Program.

JOHN H. GIBBONS, PETER D. BLAIR and **HOLLY L. GWIN** ("Strategies for Energy Use") explore energy-policy options at the Congressional Office of Technology Assessment. Gibbons has been the director of the agency for the past decade. He was educated at Randolph-Macon College and Duke University, where he got his Ph.D. in nuclear physics. Gibbons joined the Oak Ridge National Laboratory in 1954 and later directed its environmental program. Blair is manager of the energy and materials program at the agency. He earned his B.S. in engineering from Swarthmore College and his Ph.D. from the University of Pennsylvania, where he now holds an adjunct faculty appointment. Gwin is the agency's general counsel. Her undergraduate and law degrees are from the University of Tennessee.

ROBERT A. FROSCH and **NICHOLAS E. GALLO-POULOS** ("Strategies for Manufacturing") work at the General Motors Research Laboratories in Warren, Mich. Frosch, who has a Ph.D. in theoretical physics from Columbia University, has been vice-president in charge of the research laboratories at GM since 1982. Before that he was head of the National Aeronautics and Space Administration, associate director of the Woods Hole Oceanographic Institution and assistant executive director of the United Nations Environment Program. Gallopoulos is head of GM's engine research department; he was previously head of the environmental science department and assistant head of the fuels and lubricants department. Gallopoulos received his M.S. in chemical engineering from Pennsylvania State University and his B.S. from Texas A&M University.

JIM MacNEILL ("Strategies for Sustainable Economic Development") is secretary general of the World Commission on Environment and Development and a principal architect of the commission's 1986 report, "Our Common Future." He was director of environment for the Organization for Economic Cooperation and De-velopment and served as permanent secretary of the Canadian Ministry of State for Urban Affairs. He is president of MacNeill Associates and established a program on sustainable development for the Institute for Research on Public Policy in Ottawa.

WILLIAM D. RUCKELSHAUS ("Toward a Sustainable World") is chief executive officer of Browning Ferris Industries, Inc. He was administrator of the Environmental Protection Agency from 1970 to 1973 and from 1983 to 1984 and was a member of the World Commission on Environment and Development. A graduate of Princeton University and Harvard Law School, he has served as deputy attorney general of Indiana and of the U.S. and as acting director of the Federal Bureau of Investigation.

GRO HARLEM BRUNDTLAND ("Epilogue"), Prime Minister of Norway, was chairman of the World Commission on Environment and Development. She received a medical degree from Harvard University and served as Norway's minister of environment from 1974 to 1979. She became leader of her nation's Labor Party in 1981 and became prime minister in 1986.

Bibliographies

1. Managing Planet Earth

Bolin, Bert, and Robert B. Cook, eds. 1983. *The major biogeochemical cycles and their interactions.* John Wiley & Sons.

Clark, William C., and R. E. Munn, eds. 1986. *Sustainable development of the biosphere.* Cambridge University Press.

World Commission on Environment and Development. 1987. *Our common future.* Oxford University Press.

McLaren, Digby J., and Brian J. Skinner, eds. 1987. *Resources and world development.* John Wiley & Sons.

Turner, B. L., ed. 1989. *The earth as transformed by human action.* Cambridge University Press.

2. The Changing Atmosphere

World Meteorological Organization Global Ozone Research and Monitoring Project. 1985. *Atmospheric ozone 1985: Assessment of our understanding of the processes controlling its present distribution and change.* Report No. 16.

Environmental Protection Agency. 1985. *National air quality and emission trends report* Report EPA-450/4-84-029.

1986. *Acid deposition: Long-term trends.* National Academy Press.

Fay, James A., Dan Golomb and Subramanyam Kumar. 1986. Modeling of the 1900–1980 trend of precipitation acidity at Hubbard Brook, New Hampshire. *Atmospheric Environment* 20: 1825–1828.

Crutzen, P. J., and T. E. Graedel. 1986. The role of atmospheric chemistry in environment-development interactions. In *Sustainable development of the biosphere,* eds., William C. Clark and R. E. Munn. Cambridge University Press.

3. The Changing Climate

Bolin, Bert, B. R. Döös, Jill Jäger and Richard A. Warrick, eds. 1986. *The greenhouse effect, climate change, and ecosystems.* John Wiley & Sons.

Washington, Warren M., and Claire L. Parkinson. 1986. *An introduction to three-dimensional climate modeling.* University Science.

Ramanathan, V., et al. 1989. Cloud-radiative forcing and climate: Results from the earth radiation budget experiment. *Science* 243 (January 6): 57–63.

Schneider, Stephen H. 1989. *Global warming: Are we entering the greenhouse century?* Sierra Club Books.

Wigley, T. M. L. 1989. Possible climate change due to SO_2-derived cloud condensation nuclei. *Nature* 339 (June 1): 365–367.

4. Threats to the World's Water

Wicke, Lutz. 1986. *Die ökologischen milliarden.* Kosel Verlag.

McLaren, Digby L., and Brian J. Skinner, eds. 1987. *Resources and world development.* John Wiley & Sons.

World Resources Institute/International Institute for Environment and Development. 1987. *World resources 1987: An assessment of the resource base that supports the global economy.* Basic Books.

———. 1988. *World resources 1988–89: An assessment of the resource base that supports the global economy.* Basic Books.

5. Threats to Biodiversity

Raup, David M., and J. John Sepkoski, Jr. 1982. Mass extinctions in the marine fossil record. *Science* 215 (March 19): 1501–1503.

Myers, Norman. 1984. *The primary source: Tropical forests and our future.* W. W. Norton & Company.

Soulé, Michael E. ed. 1986. *Conservation biology: The science of scarcity and diversity.* Sinauer Associates, Inc.

May, Robert M. 1988. How many species are there on earth? *Science* 241 (September 16): 1441–1449.

Wilson, E. O., and Frances M. Peter, eds. 1988. *Biodiversity.* National Academy Press.

6. The Growing Human Population

Ehrlich, Paul R., Anne H. Ehrlich and John P. Holdren. 1970. *Ecoscience: Population resources, environment*. W. H. Freeman and Company.

Kelley, Allen C. 1988. Economic consequences of population change in the Third World. *Journal of Economic Literature* 26 (December): 1685–1728.

1989. *World development report, 1989*. World Bank/Oxford University Press.

7. Strategies for Agriculture

Plucknett, Donald L., and Nigel J. H. Smith. 1982. Agricultural research and Third World food production. *Science* 217 (July 16): 215–220.

Rosenberg, Norman J., Blaine L. Blad and Shashi B. Verma. 1983. *Microclimate: The biological environment*, 2nd ed. John Wiley & Sons.

Crosson, P. 1986. Agricultural development—looking to the future. In *Sustainable development of the biosphere*, eds. William C. Clark and R. E. Munn. Cambridge University Press.

Lal, Rattan. 1987. Effects of soil erosion on crop productivity. *CRC Critical Reviews in Plant Sciences* 5:303–367.

Rhoades, James D. 1987. The problem of salt in agriculture. In *1988 Yearbook of Science and the Future*. Encyclopaedia Britannica, Inc.

8. Strategies for Energy Use

Gibbons, J. H., and W. U. Chandler. 1981. *Energy: The conservation revolution*. Plenum Press.

U.S. Congress Office of Technology Assessment. 1984. *Nuclear power in an age of uncertainty*. OTA-E-216 (February).

———. 1985. *New electric power technologies: Problems and prospects for the 1990s*. OTA-E-246 (July).

Goldenberg, Jose, Thomas B. Johansson, Amulya K. N. Reddy and Robert H. Williams. 1987. *Energy for a sustainable world*. World Resources Institute.

9. Strategies for Manufacturing

Hunt, Robert G., and Richard O. Welch. 1974. *Resource and environmental profile analysis of plastics and nonplastics containers*. Midwest Research Institute.

Loebenstein, J. Roger. 1985. Platinum-group metals. *Mineral Facts and Problems*, U.S. Bureau of Mines Bulletin No. 675, U.S. Department of the Interior. U.S. Government Printing Office.

Lankford, William T., Jr., et al., eds. 1985. *The making, shaping, and treating of steel*. Association of Iron and Steel Engineers.

Ausubel, Jessee H., and Hedy E. Sladovich, eds. 1989. *Technology and environment*. National Academy Press.

Odum, Eugene P. 1989. Input management of production systems. *Science* 243 (January 13): 177–182.

10. Strategies for Sustainable Economic Development

Goldenberg, Jose, Thomas B. Johannson, Amulya K. N. Reddy and Robert H. Williams. 1985. *Energy for development*. World Resources Institute.

World Commission on Environment and Development. 1987. *Our common future*. Oxford University Press.

Brown, L. R., et al. *State of the world 1988*. W. W. Norton & Company.

Repetto, Robert, ed. 1988. *The forest for the trees? Government policies and the misuse of forest resources*. World Resources Institute.

Simonis, Udo E., et al. 1988. *Structural change and environmental policy: Empirical evidence on thirty-one countries in East and West*. Science Centre.

World Resources Institute/International Institute for Environment and Development. 1988. *World resources 1987–88: An assessment of the resource base that supports the global economy*. Basic Books.

———. 1988. *World resources 1988–89: An assessment of the resource base that supports the global economy*. Basic Books.

Pearce, David, Edward Barbier and Anil Markandya. 1989. *Sustainable development: Economics and environment in the Third World*. Edward Elgar Publishing Ltd.

11. Toward a Sustainable World

Repetto, Robert, ed. 1985. *The global possible: Resources, development, and the new century*. Yale University Press.

Gruber, Michael. 1988. *Are today's institutional tools up to the task? EPA Journal* 14 (November/December): 2–6.

Brown, Lester R., et al. 1989. *State of the world 1989*. W. W. Norton & Company.

Sources of the Photographs

Steve McCurry, Magnum Photos, Inc.: Figure 1.1

Richard O. Bierregaard, Jr., Photo Researchers, Inc.: Figure 2.1

Bruno Barbey, Magnum Photos, Inc.: Figure 2.4

Chester C. Langway, Jr., SUNY at Buffalo: Figure 2.5 (*top*)

Gary Braasch: Figure 3.1

Claude Lorius, Laboratory of Glaciology and Geophysics of the Environment: Figure 3.3

Jesse Simmons: Figure 3.7

Thase Daniel, Bruce Coleman Inc.: Figure 4.1

Ray Pfortner, Peter Arnold, Inc.: Figure 4.5

Jeff Foot, Bruce Coleman Inc.: Figure 4.7

United Nations: Figure 4.8

Ted Spiegel: Figure 4.9

Gary Braasch: Figures 5.1 and 5.5

Mark Moffett: Figure 5.2

Landsat images courtesy of Earth Observation Satellite Company, Lanham, Md.: Figure 5.6

Michael J. Balick, Peter Arnold, Inc.: Figure 5.7 (*left*)

Michael J. Balick, New York Botanical Garden: Figure 5.7 (*right*)

Sebastiano Salgado, Jr., Magnum Photos, Inc.: Figure 6.1

Hill and Knowlton: Figure 6.7

Robert Caputo: Figure 6.8

Landsat images courtesy of Earth Observation Satellite Company, Lanham, Md.: Figure 7.1

J. C. Tucker, National Aeronautics and Space Administration: Figure 7.3

World Bank: Figure 7.6

J. K. Aase, U.S. Department of Agriculture: Figure 7.7

Currey and Clark, St. Cloud, Minn.: Figure 8.1

Chris J. Calwell, Natural Resources Defense Council: Figure 8.4

Paul Logsdon: Figure 8.7

S. Varnedoe: Figure 9.1

Wellman, Inc.: Figure 9.4

George Bodenburgh, General Motors Corp.: Figure 9.5

Mark Sherman, Bruce Coleman Inc.: Figure 9.7

Co Rentmeester, The Image Bank: Figure 10.1

Raghu Rai, Magnum Photos, Inc.: Figure 10.4

International Development Research Center, Ottawa: Figure 10.6

Soviet Life: Figure 11.1

Warner Collection of the Gulf States Paper Corporation, Tuscaloosa, Ala.: Figure 11.2

Laurie Burnham: Figure 11.6

INDEX

Page numbers in *italics* indicate illustrations.